WORK, MONEY AND DUALITY
Trading Sex as a Side Hustle

Raven Bowen

Foreword by John Lowman

P

First published in Great Britain in 2021 by

Policy Press, an imprint of
Bristol University Press
University of Bristol
1-9 Old Park Hill
Bristol
BS2 8BB
UK
t: +44 (0)117 954 5940
e: bup-info@bristol.ac.uk

Details of international sales and distribution partners are available at
policy.bristoluniversitypress.co.uk

British Library Cataloguing in Publication Data
A catalogue record for this book is available from the British Library

ISBN 978-1-4473-5880-0 hardcover
ISBN 978-1-4473-5881-7 paperback
ISBN 978-1-4473-5882-4 ePub
ISBN 978-1-4473-5883-1 ePdf

Cover design: Robin Hawes
Image credit: iStock/Grandfailure

Contents

List of figures and tables

Figures

Table

Acknowledgements

I am sincerely grateful to all research participants who trusted me with their stories about living dual lives. It was a great honour to get to know each of you and to write this book as a means to safely share your experiences and insights with those who would not otherwise hear from workers like you. This work is dedicated to you, who silently juggle sex work and square jobs to support your families. You risk everything to better their lives. I especially dedicate this work in loving memory of a woman whose life ended before these stories could be shared, but it is my hope that her truth lives on in the subtext. May she rest in power.

My deepest gratitude goes to Maggie O'Neill, who set the foundation for sex work research in the UK and whose encouragement and support made this research a reality. I am deeply grateful to members of the Sex Work Research Hub and the Sociology department at Durham University for providing the PhD studentship that funded my doctorate. I also thank faculty and staff of the Sociology department at the University of York for continued funding of my PhD and for their support after my transfer from Durham.

There are extraordinary friends and family in my life who provided a counter narrative, supporting me in converting dreams to plans. I am indebted to Chris Atchison, John Lowman, Tamara O'Doherty, Raffick Bowen, Winnie Yung and Shaffiqu Bowen. Thank you, mom and dad. I am lucky to have many colleagues at National Ugly Mugs (NUM), such as Kerri Swindells, Sian Prime, Mary Laing, Laura Graham, Jewel and others who encouraged me to carve out the time necessary to write this book and thank you to the fiery community of sex workers, organisations and allies who refuse to rest until sex workers are made whole.

Special appreciation goes to Natasha 'The Kizzer' Bowen, who, in addition to creating the illustrations and animations associated with the research, remains the reason for my next breath.

Foreword

John Lowman

I met Raven Bowen in 1995, when she became a support and outreach worker at PACE Society (Prostitution Alternatives Counselling and Education) in Vancouver, British Columbia, a charitable organisation for which I served on the Board of Directors. PACE was set up in 1994 to provide housing initiatives, outreach and support services for sex workers, most of whom were survival sex workers meeting their clients on Vancouver's Downtown Eastside. Raven later become the Executive Director of PACE. From 2000 to 2006, she led the organisation to both internal program development and multi-agency collaborations, all of which were designed to improve the lives of sex workers in the Greater Vancouver Regional District and beyond.

The mid 1990s to mid 2000s were desperately sad and depressing days as they marked the zenith of the disappearances of more than 50 women from Vancouver's Downtown Eastside. We now know that Canada's most prolific serial killer had been preying on street sex workers, women about whom no one in authority gave a damn, least of all the local police. Robert 'Willy' Pickton murdered 49 sex workers, an indelible stain on Canada's reputation as a caring liberal democracy.

In 2006 and 2007, Raven served as PACE Society's Policy and Research Development Coordinator. From 2005 to 2009, she held the roles of both Regional Coordinator for the BC Coalition of Experiential Communities (BCCEC), a British Columbian policy advocacy group for sex workers. A detailed account of her work with the BCCEC can be found in Davis and Bowen (2019). Also, she was a Co-Founder of the Collaborative Research Network (CRN#6) 'Sex, Work, Law and Society', a division of the US Law and Society Association. She is former administrator of the UK Sex Work Research Hub. Since 2018, she has been the CEO of the UK's National Ugly Mugs (NUM) organisation, which seeks justice and protection for sex workers. During her time working for these organisations, she secured the equivalent of over 2 million pounds in funding for various research and service initiatives for sex workers.

In the intervening period Raven went on to complete her bachelor's and master's degrees at Simon Fraser University in Canada (Bowen, 2013) and her PhD (Bowen, 2018) at the University of York in England. Here we are some 25 years after I first met Raven reading her seminal work on 'duality', the rarely studied lives of women, men and others who work straight jobs and sex work simultaneously. 'Duality' concerns the way practitioners assimilate both their sex work and straight work into the experience of their life-world. In the process, she canvasses all of the relevant literature, which is quite an achievement given the recent growth of that literature. While the primary focus of her book is on duality, she also examines the influence of Brexit on migrant sex workers and the effect of the COVID-19 pandemic on sex workers, thus bringing her work up to date with the most recent developments of the UK 'whorearchy', the Continuum of Sex Work Involvement and the Dual-life Relational Paradigm.

Her work should remain essential reading for anyone involved in sex work research and policy making for many years to come.

References

Davis, S. and Bowen, R. (2019) 'Controlling our destinies: How the BC Coalition of Experiential Communities (BCCEC) shaped sex worker rights organising in Vancouver, British Columbia', in A. Lebovitch and S. Ferris (eds) *Sex Work Activism in Canada: Speaking Out, Standing Up*, Winnipeg, Manitoba: ARP Books, pp 139–61.

Bowen, R. (2013) 'They walk among us: sex work exiting, re-entry and duality' (MA thesis). Simon Fraser University Library Catalogue (b6258038) http://troy.lib.sfu.ca/record=b6258038~S1a.

Bowen, R. (2018) 'In plain sight: an examination of "duality", the simultaneous involvement in sex industry work and square work' (PhD thesis). University of York, UK. [Embargoed for publication until 2023] http://etheses.whiterose.ac.uk/23820/

Introduction

Part I

There is no need to look for the people whom this book is about because you probably already know them. You may work with them, or for them. These are people whom we interact with in our daily lives. They operate in plain sight. Before I tell you what this book is, I will tell you what it is not. It is not an exposé of the work and practices of a subaltern and subversive faction of deviant sex workers who manage to fool us all by also holding conventional jobs right under our noses. It is not an opportunity to gain insights in order to hunt down, name, shame and blame people who are suspected of working this way and launch witch hunts at the office because so and so showed up a little too done-up for a weekday. It is not a book containing the stories of those that one can conflate with modern day slaves, trafficking victims or vulnerable adults, exploited (in ways that differ from other workers), 'prostituted' and awaiting rescue.

Instead, this book centres on the experiences of people who live dual lives. They cannot be rescued from sex industries, reformed and delivered to mainstream jobs because they already hold them. Nor can they be convinced that leaving sex industries to take up mainstream work is salvation from 'deviant careers' or an escape from a life of sin. They take on the paid work available to them within our precarious labour markets, so no, they are not sex workers exploited by pimps and madams, who can be 'saved' in the ways that we are led to believe are necessary through sensationalised misinformation campaigns. In truth, they are indistinguishable from other mainstream workers and cannot be bamboozled into romanticised constructs of square work, and a sole reliance upon it, as being the best way to earn a quality standard of living. Some of them have struggled to survive on benefits and Universal Credit, they have suffered through 10 years of austerity and workfare policies. They drank the Kool-Aid™ and with an established belief in a just world, went to university to get training for good paying jobs to raise families and contribute to the economy. They pose a formidable challenge to representations of sex workers because they defy stereotypes about who sex industry workers can *be*.

These individuals are among some of the most hidden off-street and online workers in the population. They are silenced because they cannot openly discuss their sex working yet through this research they contribute an immense amount to our understandings of labour markets and precarisation. Contributors provide insights into mainstream working conditions and informal economies, particularly sex industries; plural identities and role transition; and stigma and secret keeping. Sex industry workers and their markets are influenced by mainstream economies, geopolitics, stratification, systems of domination, and for these workers, vice versa. What happens in one market reverberates in the other and their experiences existing in both can greatly expand our comprehension about sex work and society. Our approaches to designing interventions may altogether shift to favour collaborations that meaningfully involved active sex workers instead of being almost entirely guided by the experiences of non-sex workers and those with experiences in the sex industries of yesteryear. This is not to say that former sex workers and those who define themselves as 'survivors' do not have a lot of insights to contribute to shaping policy and services in this regard, they do. I argue that active sex workers must be first in the queue to inform the design of policy interventions geared towards improving their well-being and reducing the harm and exploitation they experience.

In this book, I retell their stories and in doing so I tell ours.

In this chapter

In this Introduction, relevant terms are defined and the central research question, ethical considerations, methodology and theoretical approach will be presented, along with some commentary on the size and elusiveness of off-street sex industries. Additionally, literature that points to what is known about duality will be shared. Our journey to find these dual-life sex workers will take us back to the 19th century, where poor women did their best to make ends meet though unemployment and policy environments that targeted their enterprising activities. Following this, I summarise the debates about sex as work within feminisms that help make sense of the subjugated positioning of people who trade sex, particularly street-based workers. The treatment and plight of sex workers is then associated with deeply rooted class conflict and fights for representation, resources and respect. Part II introduces contributors by way of demographics, skills and some frustrations that they experience, and ends with a description of book chapters ahead.

—

Sex work is the commercial exchange of sexual products, services and performances for money or goods where consenting adults negotiate the details of these transactions. These details include pricing, services, duration, location and other terms necessary for contracting and a meeting of minds. The term 'sex work' was coined in the late 1970s by Carol Leigh aka Scarlot Harlot, who wanted the labour aspects of the provision of sexual and intimate services to be recognised. I use the term sex work in this book to reflect and respect how contributors define their activities across marketplaces. I define sex work as work, sex workers as workers and recognise their participation in the legal economic activity of selling sexual services in the UK. The term 'prostitution' only appears in quoted content and when referring to historical contexts and legislation because many sex workers feel this language is derogatory. I refer to forced labour in sex industries as 'survival sex', where individuals have little opportunity to refuse work and express few options to make the money that they need to stay alive. People in both sex work and survival sex operate under conditions of stigma and experience various forms of violence, hard-targeting and criminalisation, which reduces their safety, power and autonomy.

The term 'square' is better known in North America, where my original research on transitioning and duality is based. It refers to non-sex work jobs, people who have left sex industries and those who have never been involved. Many contributors used the term 'straight'. Some referred to their square jobs and lives as 'real', 'civvy', 'regular', 'vanilla', 'mainstream', 'conventional' and 'normal'. Some referred to their sex industry work as their 'hooker job'.

Taking the sex work is work standpoint will place this book in opposition to radical, carceral and prohibitionist perspectives on sex working that characterise it as wholly exploitative. I agree with the stated views of some feminists related to how systems of patriarchy, capitalism, colonialism and other power structures oppress women, challenge their fair access to resources and limit opportunities for their advancement in society. I disagree that the way forward towards eliminating women's subjugation in survival sex is to disrespect how adults may identify and define their contexts and behaviours. Sex work and square work are defined by contributors as work that is both liberating and exploitive because work itself is dynamic, lives are complex and labour markets are constantly in flux. As a researcher my role is to report on lived experiences, discover nuance and critically expand the relevant ways that sex work is discussed and understood. I make space in this book for those living dual lives, who do not have a safe platform to share their experiences and little opportunity to shape discourse and policy. Their exclusion is due in part to how sex workers are mischaracterised by those with political power, who use their privilege to influence decisions about who gets heard from on this issue and who is dismissed.

Duality

> Out beyond ideas of wrongdoing and rightdoing, there is a field, I'll meet you there.
>
> (Rumi)[1]

The term 'duality' denotes two aspects,[2] 'a situation of nature that has two states or parts that are complementary or opposed to each other'.[3] Philosophers such as Plato, Plutarch and Rumi often discussed essential questions about the purpose of being as linked to dualisms between good and evil, material and non-material, light and shadow, right and wrong. Here, the term describes work across sex industries and square work and is in part a rejection of other terminology such as 'secret life' or 'double life' that hold negative connotations. Sex industry work is already stigmatised, and framing the practices of blending work across these fields in a negative way, a 'secret life' for example, is not in the spirit of the research.

Within the context of this book, duality is an innovative set of practices undertaken by workers within diverse labour markets. Managing concurrent sex work and square work requires courage and relies upon entrepreneurialism, privilege and skill, all of which are elements necessary for success in today's gigging economy. Having a series of 'side hustles', 'transition hustles', temporary jobs, casual work alongside more stable work or mainstream employment with income from informal economies has become the new normal, no doubt due in part to deskilling and casualisation, with unequal distribution of capital and the primacy of materialism in our society. Sex work and square work can be interpreted as polar, oppositional, disparate, but this would be a mistake. People who live dual work lives manage plural identities between work and personal lives, as we all do, and compartmentalise sex work and square work to avoid stigma. They exist appropriately in all fields of interaction. The work that they take on may be lived as more complementary. Representations of sex work as something that one is either in or out of, trapped in or having survived, provides little acknowledgement of what is entailed in how these worlds can overlap and avoids some of the most compelling arguments for anti-stigma and anti-oppression initiatives by, with and for sex industry workers.

4

I met these sex workers who live dual lives in the context of research, and they are tax-paying employees, entrepreneurs, innovators and content creators in their worlds of work. I will refer to them as 'contributors' from here on because they give. They give to our economies and workforces, to their families and loved ones, and they are part of who we are. They await us in a field, a liminal space between binaries and we shall meet them there.

Ethics and anonymity

Contributors are an elusive population of on- and off-street and online sex workers who hide their involvement in sex work to safeguard against being 'outed'. They must avoid the stigma and discrimination that comes with people knowing what they do. *Sub Rosa* sex work is done to conceal their identities, even from others in sex industries, and of course in their square jobs because intentional or accidental revelation exposes them to a *social taint* (Hughes, 1958). They stand to lose everything: relationships, status, prospects, employment, housing and more, because the effects of 'whore stigma' are life changing. Access to these hidden workers was granted through advertising in online forums as well as a referral-snowballing technique made possible through relationships established with sex working communities over the past couple of decades. Potential contributors could search my background and make informed decisions about whether to trust me with their secrets as many told no one else about their dual lives and they had a lot at stake.

Although the research received ethics approval first at Durham University in April 2016 and shortly afterwards at the University of York, meeting standard ethics requirements in sociology for research with human subjects, it was paramount that evidence such as contributors' quotes and stories be presented in ways that prevented the reverse engineering of biographies. One sex worker who later became a contributor read my MA study on transitioning and duality among off-street sex workers in Vancouver, British Columbia. She asked me not to present demographic information with pseudonyms in a chart form. Other contributors requested that their demographic information and quoted content not be linked. As a compromise, and to improve readability, some quoted content will be referenced as 'Anonymous' instead of with the associated pseudonym to reduce the risk of this book outing contributors. Information is presented in aggregate form where possible, which may be challenging to read as many would like to cross-reference biographical information with ethnographic material, but this is the price we pay to hear from this population because stigma kills.

The approach to data collection was inspired by interpretive phenomenological analysis (IPA). IPA is a reflexive interviewing technique that allows contributors to describe and interpret their experiences in response to prompts that facilitated the democratic co-production of knowledge. The goal of phenomenological research is to capture a complete description of lived experience to find meaning and understand behaviours in context (Englander, 2012). IPA is respectful and democratic because 'in phenomenological research initial reflection is by the person who has undergone a particular experience, and this reflection is a primary interpretation' (Bevan, 2014, p 137).

Contributors' reflections of their duality were important to document because the research was not about exposing their strategies but instead about sharing the meaning behind their behaviours towards a greater understanding of their lives. Phenomenological interviews involve: *contextualisation*, through obtaining details of an experience; an *apprehending of the phenomenon* by asking questions that uncover the meaning behind human action; and *clarifying the phenomenon*, through careful analysis (Englander, 2012).

In total, 36 phenomenological interviews were conducted among 35 contributors (one UK contributor was interviewed twice) where 'thick descriptions' (Geertz, 1973) of transitioning and duality were gathered. Twenty-five (n=25) contributors reside in the UK and are the focus of this book and the remaining contributors reside in Canada. Interviews took place between 2016 and 2018 and ranged in length from one hour to 5.5 hours.

Research question and methodology

The research that informs this book was exploratory in nature and was shaped by a core research question that simply asked: 'What is the nature of duality?' Examining duality as part of, but distinct from, transitioning is the core contribution of this research. This broad line of questioning was useful in mapping practices and the insights of people who work at the intersection of sex industry work and square work (SIWSQ). Their experiences inform a Continuum of SIWSQ Involvement that provides a framework to organise a range of practices such as intermittent sex working; strategic involvement in sex industries; sustained duality; opportunistic and experimental dabbling in sex work or square work; and 'sexiting', where people may engage in either kind of work as a means to 'exit' or transition (Bowen,

2013). Foundational to the inquiry was discovering how individuals managed discrediting information, segregated audiences (both on- and offline) and transitioned between stigmatised and mainstream roles. The Dual-life Relational Paradigm and the Continuum of SIWSQ Involvement are the central means of conceptualising duality. Contributors discussed the benefits, risks and challenges of living a dual life and the factors that influenced their working arrangements, such as the precarious labour market and Brexit.

Theoretical approach to studying duality

Theoretical approaches advanced in this book to better understand duality draw insights from conflict theories and Marx's alienation and estrangement, as well as relational sociology, as means to transcend dualisms of structure/agency; subject/object; macro/micro; individual/society – or in this case, binary categorisations of good/bad, victim/deviant, in/out, Madonna/whore, and sex work/square work. There is also a need to avoid codeterministic *both/and* intersectional approaches (originated by Crenshaw (1991) and canonised by Hill-Collins (1990) and others) to explain what contributors are doing. Ego-centred codeterministic approaches to conceptualisations of human action as *volunteerism* (agency-structure) and *determinism* (structure-action) are part of a dialectic of agency and structure or 'structured agency' (Dépelteau, 2008). From this perspective, individuals act (biography, disposition) as expected within contexts and over time (history and culture) and these actions become reified (structure), yet: 'the actor forgets that the institution exists only through their actions' (Dépelteau, 2008, p 53).

Capitalism, patriarchy and colonialism are constructs of human action. More precisely, a non-material social form such as class is not something imposed, but an activity that is *done* (Veenstra and Burnett, 2014). As such, class inequity is done by us. The social phenomenon of duality is part of a web of irreducible relations and trans-actions engaged in by actors in environments that we all have a hand in creating. The social structures that some are oppressed by are 'chains of trans-action' (Dépelteau, 2008, p 62). They are of people doing things, repeatedly. King (1999) suggests that structure is just *other people* and social processes (Dépelteau, 2008). Relational sociology eliminates the compulsion to reduce the pressures felt by people into individualised or reified dimensions, thus helping us here to associate formal and informal markets, putting sex work *in relation* to square work, and sex workers *in relation* to other workers.

Social environments, although possessing some proscriptive elements, are budding with possibilities for self-representation, misrepresentation, trans-action and (in)action. Drawing inspiration from Schütz's (1967) approach to phenomenology and conceptualisation of our life-worlds being made meaningful through social action, there exists an 'intersubjectivity', not individuals acting in environments, but people transacting and creating a social reality, a lived experience. Goffman posits our social world is comprised of situations that hold 'a matrix of possible events and a cast of roles through whose enactment ... constitute together a field for fateful dramatic action ... an engine of meaning ... different from all other worlds except the ones generated when the same game is played' (1961, p 25). Sex working, then, is part of a realm of possibilities that persons co-create, which makes it absurd in the phenomenological sense, to judge or ostracise people for trading sex as it is a form of work that we have co-constructed.

The 'game' Goffman refers to is the expectations, structures and order of an encounter as influenced by the setting. Moreover, if we accept Schütz's conceptualisation of the life-world comprising 'modes of knowledge' or Bourdieu's account of field, as a site of interaction where various forms of (social, economic, cultural and symbolic) capitals are negotiated based on the stakes and profits available within overlapping contexts (Bourdieu, 1986; Bourdieu and Wacquant, 1992) then we can view social interactions as irreducible units of meaning. Environments and behaviour, action and reason, are interdependent and co-created. In this relational framework, once what is meaningful is identified, we can come to understand the dialectics and logic behind practices, and how behaviours reproduce the environments that circumscribe human action (Wacquant, 1990). Sex work as a phenomenon can transcend victim/whore (deviant) binaries and structure-agency debates. Duality can be understood beyond sex work and square work and beyond individual identity because relational field theory eliminates 'substantialist thinking' (Veenstra and Burnett, 2014). As a result, duality is conceptualised as a series of strategic and sometimes overlapping relations and practices mapped across life-worlds in sex work and square work, instead of as disparate work environments that people toggle between, or as a phenomenon that is agential or structural in nature. Decisions about sex work and square work involvement are informed by one's 'stock of experience' (Schütz, 1967), their biographies, internalised structure, *habitus* and dispositions that incorporate history, past motivations and future goals.

We live in a phenomenological life-world with multiple valances, where people construct the field through their own movements that are intrinsic to the field and other actors (Martin, 2003). Duality is inextricably linked to social structures, conflict, actors and trans-actions within dynamic environments. The trans-actions associated with work itself, irrespective of whether it involves sexual services, occur within 'fields of organized striving' (Martin, 2003, p 20) where internally logical social environments comprise actors, these contributors, oriented towards common rewards such as the resources for life. Duality as human 'trans-action' is at the macro level, social conflict, class struggle and a competition for resources that are (re)produced in the tensions and complexities of environments among those 'striving' for economic security. People 'whether strategic or norm following, are inseparable from the transactional contexts within which they are embedded' (Emirbayer, 1997, p 287). Sex work cannot be separated out from capitalism, market transactions or our mainstream economy, just as sex workers cannot be excised from other labourers because, in the case of these contributors, they are one and the same.

How many sex workers? No idea!

Dare I say nobody has any idea how many sex workers are active at any given time in the UK. There are extrapolations and educated (or otherwise) 'guestimations' that vary widely. Due to criminalisation, stigma and the value of being discreet, sex workers who can avoid being public will do so and publicised numbers are often misleading and politically motivated. Based on the number of sex workers accessing services in the registry of the UK Network of Sex Work Projects (circa 2007–8), now National Ugly Mugs, researchers estimated the entire population in the UK and Scotland at the time to be approximately 36,000 with a multiplier of three, compared with another publicised number of 80,000 in 1999 by Cusick et al (2009). Both of these estimates may be incorrect and are shaped by how people are counted, who is counted and also who is *doing* the counting. Populations such as migrants, workers of colour, parents, those living dual lives, seniors, students and others will remain largely undetected because there is no benefit to coming out or participating in research. There is a perception that doing so will only serve to sharpen the blunt instruments of the state, to penalise or oppress sex workers with a precision that is informed by research about their populations. The activities of colonial anthropologists had similar outcomes for tribal populations throughout the world.

The Home Office commissioned research by Hester et al (2019) of Bristol University that was recommended by the Home Affairs Select

9

committee in 2016. This research aimed to uncover the nature and prevalence of sex work and develop typologies and estimations of populations in the UK. The total subsample of sex workers included 529 people, with 42 completing follow-up in-depth surveys. The study provided no new insights into the prevalence of sex work in the UK and restated the concerns of many in this regard that 'producing unbiased estimates requires a (sufficiently large) representative sample ... the nature of sex work and the stigma often associated with it means that activities often occur in private' (Hester et al, 2019). Hester et al also state that 'any attempt at estimating the prevalence of prostitution and sex work will require the cooperation of a wide range of actors. Different actors are aware of, and in contact with, different segments of the market' (2019, p 40). In the end, they echo Sanders et al (2018) who previously identified the issues with counting sex workers.

While determining the exact number of people working in sex industries may not be possible, the proportion of on- and off-street sex workers has been estimated due to visibility. For example, Lowman and Atchison (2006) note that street-based sex workers comprise up to 20 per cent of the sex working population in Canada. It is safe to say that off-street and online workers comprise the bulk of sex industry workers in the UK as a comparable society, and account for the low numbers of sex workers visible at street level. This is a trend that is set to increase given the virtual en masse transition of many industries (particularly sales) to the digital environment as a result of technological advancements and more recently due in part to the COVID-19 pandemic of 2019–21. Most of the work available in sex industries is mediated through tech and many workplaces exist off-street and online. Off-street sex industry workers take on various career paths as masseuses, dancers, adult film actors, full and partial sexual service providers, models, webcammers, doms and dommes, and pro subs, to name a few, and they may engage in this work concurrently (Orchard et al, 2012).

There are several research studies about off-street sex workers that help construct a portrait. One early study observed 'outlaw broads' (Bryan, 1965, p 288) who worked as independents and shared best practices and strategies to avoid exploitation by clients, pimps and managers. Many took full advantage of educational resources, their class positions and all the benefits brought about by the sexual revolution (contraceptives, divorce, and so on) or 'plastic sexuality' (Giddens, 1991) that disassociates sex from procreation. As early as the 1990s, those working as off-street escorts were noted as moving out of service industry and public sector careers in response to poor wages.

Off-street workers fall along a spectrum of socio-economic levels, including both working class and elite workers (Bernstein, 2007). There appears to be an ordinariness to off-street sex work among populations of independent workers as well. This was captured by Hoigard and Finstad (1992) who interviewed 26 working class and 'lumpenproletariat' women who had experienced economic instability and institutionalisation, but were acknowledged as 'a neglected group of women ... more of them off-street workers from middle-class backgrounds, who exercise conscious choice in turning to sex work' (Scambler and Scambler, 1997, p 113). Further, Scambler and Scambler itemised five key misconceptions of who trades sex that likely hold true today. Among them are that sex workers are heterogeneous populations, they are not passive victims, they have ethical standards and practices to protect their own health and safety and that of their clients, and they are skilled labourers who challenge patriarchy by innovating through 'norm-breaking'.

Contemporary samples of off-street sex workers most relevantly in the UK and Canada comprise diverse populations who identify across age, culture/race, gender and all socio-economic levels as seen here (Scambler and Scambler, 1997; Scambler, 2007; O'Neill et al, 2010; Law, 2013; Bowen, 2015; O'Doherty, 2015; Ham and Gilmour, 2017; O'Neill et al, 2017; Raguparan, 2017; Campbell et al, 2018). Although research on off-street sex workers tends to be based on purposive or convenience sampling strategies, some characteristics are emerging. These workers are often between 30 and 60 years of age. Their educational attainment is notable, with roughly 30 per cent or more holding university qualifications. Many possess broad work experience in sex work, providing a wide range of sexual services across venues as well as work experience in jobs in the public, private and third sectors. In the case of those living dual lives, these work experiences are concurrent (Bowen, 2013; Pitcher, 2018). It is unclear at this point if off-street workers in the UK and Canada comprise an overrepresentation of people of colour relative to the general population.

Dollymop

To bring history and context to understanding the contributors to this book, a look back to manifestations of duality in recent history is an important step. Employment opportunities for women with limited skills and for those in markets that undervalue their work was an issue in the 19th century and remains one today. Jane Addams (1895) documents the experiences of women involved in the disorganised sewing trades in Chicago (Lemert, 2004). Women of Hull-House in Chicago eked out a living on meagre wages. He states: 'no trades are so overcrowded as the sewing-trades; for the needle have ever been the refuge of the unskilled woman' (Lemert, 2004, p 69). With the scarcity of paid work in gendered trades or pink ghettos, references to duality (but not by this term) appear in the 19th century and are associated with poor and working class women. Milliners, hatmakers and other women of this period no doubt had unpredictable and potentially seasonal incomes and were known to sell sex. O'Neill writes: '... poor women sold sex in Victorian England to survive, and many sold sex in addition to their "day" jobs, for which they earned a pittance' (O'Neill, 2010, p 213). Similarly, Mayhew (1861) documented the available work among the poor in 19th-century London. He writes that orphaned girls who were mud-larks (poor children and adults who searched for valuables and fragments of materials, such as clay pipes, on riverbanks that they could trade for food) transitioned to prostitution because, in comparison, it was 'easy' and 'lucrative'.

Tait, a 19th-century Scottish physician who sought to determine the nature and extent of prostitution, compared the on-street sex industry in America and France with the more 'respectable' off-street manifestation in his city of Edinburgh. In his 1840 manuscript, he lists reasons for prostitution that include: *natural causes* such as irritability, the desire to dress well (especially among the lower classes), the desire for sexual gratification or to own property; and *accidental causes* such as bad marriages, poverty, low pay in women's work, the lack of adequate education, and of course, 'theatre-going'. He acknowledges that women participated in selling sex for money and social advancement. He writes: 'The temptation of money alone is a great inducement for females to resort to a life of prostitution ... the hope of being one day such an honoured person is a still stronger motive for their joining the ranks of vice' (Tait, 1840, p 146).

Accounts ascribe deviancy to women who concealed their supplemental sex work. Tait counts among these off-street workers, private harlots, and mistresses, those who: 'keep up a show of industry, as domestics, sempstresses, nurses, and so on , in the most respectable families ...' (Tait, 1840, p 6). He estimates that one third of all servants were 'sly prostitutes', who were very selective about their clientele and concealed their real names from the men they saw to avoid being detected. He writes: 'their object in preferring strangers is that they run less chance of being detected in their evil conduct, and that they may use greater liberties, and be enabled also to conceal their own names' (p 8) but who nonetheless 'deliver themselves up to this wicked life' (p 6).

The situation in New York City in the 19th century was no different for young women (Gilfoyle, 1987). Gilfoyle notes that 'males of the city provided a ready clientele for prostitutes, gender discrimination in the "free market" gave young women few opportunities for economic advancement. Prostitution was, in large part, based on the impoverishment of working-class women' (Gilfoyle, 1987, p 384).

Hemynge, whose original work was published in 1967, revealed that in London, by 1860, there were an estimated 80,000 sex workers, who were comprised of three categories: women kept by men as mistresses; independent women working in apartments; and women who worked in brothels (Hemynge, 2003). The second group worked in apartments, were more educated than brothel-based workers and participated in other forms of work. Hemynge documents: 'A large number of milliners, dress-makers, furriers, hat-binders … or those who work for cheap tailors, those in pantry-cooks, fancy and cigar shops … are more or less prostitutes and patronesses of the numerous brothels London can boast of possessing' (Hemynge, 2003, p 48).

More evidence of duality appears in *Green's Dictionary of Slang*, which defines Dollymop as 'part-time prostitutes, often a servant or shopgirl, esp. a milliner who occas. sells her body to supplement her otherwise meagre income' (Green, 2020). Noted British sex historian, Kate Lister, author of the 2020 book *A Curious History of Sex*, confirms the use of this term to mean a woman who sells sex alongside other jobs. Working class women, who fell in love with soldiers and who earned low wages in manufacturing and service industry jobs were seen as 'more or less prostitutes'. A recent book entitled *The Five: The Untold Stories of the Women Killed by Jack the Ripper* shares important details about the lives of five poor working class women (Polly, Annie, Elizabeth, Catherine and Mary Jane) and references 'casual prostitution' and 'dollymop' (Rubenhold, 2019). Rubenhold writes: 'In the eyes of society, and the army, Ruth had become a "dollymop": a soldier's woman who, while not quite falling into the category of "professional", was deemed a sort of "amateur" prostitute' (Rubenhold, 2019, p 92).

Although it is clear that poor wages and the limited opportunities for survival for women inspired sex work and duality, their innovations were nonetheless framed as sinful and deceitful: 'The members of the family are no sooner to bed than she unlocks the door, and walks the street as a common woman, or goes to fulfil appointments previously made with gentlemen … girls who are guilty of this bad conduct are sure to ultimately become open prostitutes' (Tait, 1840, p 122). The idea that working class women who engaged in duality would then be trapped in sex industries full time was seeded and the rationale of low wages or unemployment was successfully deflected.

Poor sex workers were the folk devils, who put society's institutions, mores and even its health in jeopardy. The most visible sex workers are targeted first through moral judgements, gender oppression, law and policy that serve to shame, criminalise and displace. Walkowitz (1977) examined employment options available to women in Plymouth and Southampton in the 19th century in the context of the 1866 Contagious Disease Act. Employment available to women in these regions included surface jobs at mines and employment as servants, laundresses and dressmakers. Women engaged in duality as they 'may have found the shorter hours and better pay of prostitution a temporary and relatively attractive solution to their immediate difficulties' (Walkowitz, 1977, p 76). Sadly, the Contagious Disease Act gathered intelligence on these kinds of workers and subjected them to genital examinations to stop the spread of sexually transmitted infections to 'middle-class sons' (Diduck and Wilson, 2003), thus creating a division, however thin, between sex workers and other working class women. The 19th and 20th centuries had an almost exclusive focus on the most visible street-based trade in the UK. Sex workers were *managed* (displaced and criminalised) through the 1824 Vagrancy Act, and various incarnations of the Contagious Disease Acts (1864, 1866 and 1869), and later regulated through the 1956 Sexual Offences Act. In 1957 the Wolfenden Committee, who were charged with investigating prostitution, produced a report that had some progressive elements, such as the decriminalisation of homosexuality (Sanders, 2012), but framed street-based sex work as a violation of decency and a public nuisance. Many believe that these sentiments lead to increased harms to sex workers.

Much of the literature on casual and part-time workers comes out of health research that positions part-time sex workers as most likely responsible for the spread of diseases such as HIV due to the clandestine nature of their work or the lack of recognition of their sexual activities as sex work (Harcourt and Donovan, 2005). Aral et al (2003) similarly drew a link between part-time sex work and the spread of HIV after the fall of the Soviet Union when there was increasing poverty and social inequality. Gysels et al (2002) conducted a study among 34 women in a Uganda trading town. The sex workers who lived dual lives, who worked square jobs as waitresses or who owned the very bars they worked in, had lower rates of HIV infection. Concurrent sex work and square work can be opportunistic sexual exchanges, where sexual acts are not premeditated (Harcourt and Donovan, 2005), or incidental, where the individuals who trade sex do not engage in it for money or identify as sex workers per se (Morris, 2018). Duality, however, is a set of practices engaged in for the purposes of earning money. It has been noted in several studies but not examined in depth: 'soft prostitution' (Mishra and Neupane, 2015); 'parallel employment trajectories' (Law, 2013); 'overlapping orientations' (Lucas, 2005); and most recently 'dual career trajectories' (Ham and Gilmour, 2017), a study that draws on my 2013 research.

Brents et al (2010) document duality during the rise of leisure economies in Nevada, noting that mining camps contained bars, restaurants and saloons, churches, housing and post offices and that they were hubs for relatively well-paid miners. The emergence of prostitution was part of forming the leisure industry in 19th-century Nevada, where saloons were the nexus of mining towns, integrating sex, alcohol, gambling, entertainment and housing (Brents et al, 2010). Single women gravitated to booming mining towns and 'prostitution' was a commonly disclosed occupation in Virginia City Nevada. Not so different from their Ugandan counterparts, most women by 1870 worked as sex workers alongside industrial and service industry jobs and other enterprises common to the women of the era. These working class women were part of the process of urbanisation.

In her riveting account of sex tourism in the Caribbean, Kempadoo (1999) describes how white slave owners would send domestic slaves (black and mixed-heritage women) to plantations and ships to work as prostitutes. Slave owners exploited and benefited from women of colour through both their physical *and* sexual labour. Traditional employment for Caribbean women such as midwifery and nursing, and as nannies and housemaids were all roles where women concurrently engaged in sex work (Kempadoo, 1999). Blending sex work with other jobs, for women in the Caribbean, was a path to emancipation for some. Caribbean women strategically laboured selling sex as part of economic transnational relationships, that is tourism. Women engaged in 'multiple sources of livelihood' and 'multiple and interrelated occupations' (Kempadoo 1999). They worked in bars, selling weed, as housekeepers, and in mixed formal and informal sector work to establish businesses of their own and support their families.

Other accounts of duality, among women of colour, include research by Ocha and Earth (2013), who interviewed Asian *Kathoey* or transgender workers whose semi-gender reassigned bodies constituted emergent sexual identities in the context of expanding global markets. These workers sold sex directly, full time and deliberately; or indirectly and part time and opportunistically, alongside schooling, jobs in retail and art-based economies (Ocha and Earth, 2013). Sex working is lucrative for women, particularly when done alongside other jobs. Sanders and Hardy (2013) surveyed 197 dancers in the UK and found that 45 per cent (n=109) held other jobs outside of the sex industry. Most recently, Pitcher's (2018) sample of 40 indoor workers included nine who lived dual lives, who ran businesses, worked in healthcare and retail, and did office work.

Drawing on these historical and contemporary accounts of overlapping employment in (in)formal economies, this practice of duality is situated within the culture of capitalism in ways authentic to how it is lived. This is in line with Bernstein (2007), who rightly recommends that we must take a synoptic view of the sex industry as inextricably linked to capitalism, the expansion of service work and the commodification of all things. The semptresses and sly prostitutes of Tait's generation are likely to be driven by the same constraints that motivate entrepreneurialism among workers, sex workers and those living dual lives today.

The debate about whether sex ought to be traded for money or other benefits rages on in the lives of contributors and in the foreground of this book and is the preoccupation of some scholars, politicians, feminists, lawmakers and other (mostly state) actors who have the power to set priorities and interventions in keeping with their ideologies and agendas. Some radical feminists police the sexuality of other adult women by pushing for prohibition and carceral feminism approaches (Musto, 2010; Bernstein, 2010, 2019) to eliminate sex industries through criminalisation despite the harms caused by these strategies. They utilise police and enforcement resources to irresponsibly disrupt sex industries and force 'exit' yet provide no comprehensive support packages commensurate with women's earnings in sex industries.

Criminalising sex workers 'for their own good' puts them in desperate situations, making them poorer, more reliant on third parties and on potential exploiters, and forces them to compromise their health and safety to make money. Carceral and radical feminists, for example, argue that women's bodies are not workplaces and ought not be 'sold' yet ignore the fact that many occupations require people to sell their bodies for money, such as modelling, policing, the armed forces, acting, dance, professional sports and several others. Many of us sell our physical and intellectual labour for money, putting our bodies and brains on the line. One radical feminist journalist even stated that 'if sex work is work then rape is theft' (Bindel, 2018). I disagree, rape is rape. If a boxer does not consent to a match and gets punched in the face, that is not boxing it is assault. Adults consent, they make choices about what they are willing to do with their bodies and minds to make money, although these are often constrained choices. Some may not agree with sex as a form of work, but we ought to respect the hustle and the dire situations that members of our communities experience. Our task is to eliminate forced labour in all of its manifestations and find ways for people to make what they determine to be freer, more liberated choices about work.

Unfortunately, some privileged women lobbyists, journalists and conservative politicians often speak for, about and instead of active sex workers. For example, Scotland's Equally Safe national strategy (Scottish Government, 2018) aims to prevent 'all forms of violence against women and girls' yet excludes sex workers from active participation in achieving this aim. In May of 2020, Umbrella Lane, a well-known and trusted sex worker support organisation, was barred from COVID-19 emergency funding through the Scottish government because they support the autonomy of sex workers.[4] Their organisation, founded in 2015, provides services to over 500 sex workers in Scotland and includes those who are exploited as well as those who choose sex work as a job or career. This inclusivity was weaponised by women in power and effectively blocked Umbrella Lane from a multi-agency approach that would get resources to sex workers during the pandemic. The violence that underpins excluding these sex workers and the organisations they trust from benefiting from state resources is a form of victimisation often ignored. The voices of professional service providers, former sex workers and those who identify as 'survivors' are important but cannot be a replacement for the meaningful involvement of active sex workers who need support now.

Would that Umbrella Lane's experience of sex worker-exclusionary politics be an isolated incident. Sadly, it is not. Public funds were denied to Sex Workers Alliance of Ireland (SWAI) for COVID-19 response to sex workers by the Department of Justice because, in service to their diverse population of sex workers and their commitments to inclusivity, SWAI has not declared sex work as inherently exploitative (Kelleher, 2020). This may be accurate for some, but it is inaccurate as a generalisation. Furthermore, sex work can be unsafe for some due to the working conditions, socio-legal policy environments and contexts such as having no access to (state or other) resources when the market goes bust and the denial of rights and control over the sex industry itself. SWAI had to rely on crowd funding for the 160 sex workers who contacted them in dire need. Some of these sex workers are taxpayers too and in their hour of need the organisations that they trust the most are prevented from providing support due to petty politics. This is not justice. The United Nations states that the criminalisation and discrimination of sex workers around the world must end and it lists a range of measures, including greater partnerships with sex worker organisations, income supports and an end to evictions and raids (UNAIDS, April 2020). The COVID-19 pandemic presents an opportunity for all of us, including our political representatives from across ideologies, to show leadership and humanity, to transcend divides to save the lives of marginalised people in our communities, even if we disagree with them.

People have the right to an opinion about who trades sex, but not everyone has the right to inform policy. Initiatives to set standards ought to be based on weighted evidence from active lived experience, insights from practitioners, findings from scholarly research and information from professionals in adult care, health and public protection, for example. States that adopt asymmetrical criminalisation, such as Ireland under the Criminal Law (Sexual Offences) Act 2017, which makes it illegal to buy sex but not to sell sex, perpetuate de facto criminalisation of sex workers, leading to their impoverishment and victimisation. Their intentions may be to save women, but this rescue is done without a lifeline to access liveable wages, housing, education and other resources. Policies like this not only thrust sex workers into poverty, they guarantee that they are not engaged as equal stakeholders in shaping solutions. This privileges women with power to *talk over* sex workers and deny calls for inclusive representation, rights and recognition. At times, people who sell sex are positioned as victims of their own poor decisions and character. 'Whore stigma' (Pheterson, 1993) shames sex workers for selling sex for monetary gain. They are framed as 'other', as a nuisance and as a threat to our society. Sadly, these are the same workers who experience high rates of harm by predators, serial killers and other dangerous individuals.

If sex workers were treated as victims, the most marginalised among them, street-based workers, would experience the greatest protections. Instead they are regularly hard-targeted by some resident groups, with discriminatory and stigma-inciting names such as 'Save our Eyes'[5] that enlist councils and police to enforce punitive and criminogenic policies to fine and displace people for engaging in behaviours associated with survival sex. Fining and incarcerating sex workers has never made sense to me because we know that poor women (and others) trade sex for money for basic needs and to ask them to pay into state coffers too is abhorrent. Carceral feminists are against the objectification of women's bodies through patriarchy and the 'use' of women as commodities within capitalism; yet, there is little outrage at the relegation of sex workers to the edges of our communities or the caging of the female body through heavy-handed enforcement policies informed by end demand and anti-sex work ideologies. There is no outcry from radical feminists about the invisibilisation of the legitimate interests of active sex workers in policy decisions affecting their lives as people most affected. Hull, for example, resuscitated the 1972 Local Government Act, section 222 in 2014. Its aim was to hard-target and displace sex workers from public sight. Thankfully, due to pressures applied by interest groups, the High Court of Justice overturned this injunction on 10 June 2020, despite it being recently touted as a successful tool in banning the street-based sex industry in Hull by Council members and law enforcement.[6] Reviving a 48-year-old policy to stop street-based sex work in modern Britain is an extreme and oppressive non-solution that harms poor women trading sex in that community and thankfully the High Court agreed. Resources could have been better spent addressing poverty among this population but there seems to be no political will to do so.

Sex workers experience *symbolic stigma* (Herek et al, 2005) whereby groups already disliked are tied to elements that pose a threat to society. This is because of pairing sex workers with societal harms such as crime, public nuisance, disease and moral corruption, while there is little investment in their well-being. Lowman's famous concept of the 'discourse of disposal' (2000, p 1003) highlights co-conspirators: media, law enforcement and communities, that worked in concert and without involvement of sex workers to 'improve' safety in neighbourhoods by displacing the visible sex industry to the industrial areas of Vancouver British Columbia in the 1980s and 1990s (Lowman, 2000). This created environments for predatory violence that contributed to the high rates of victimisation and murder experienced by street-level sex workers. Sex workers were 60 to 120 times more likely to be victims of violence (Lowman and Fraser, 1995). These moves to dispose of street-based sex workers, leaving them susceptible to murder and other harms, continues to occur in many jurisdictions. Sex workers are not treated as members of our communities deserving of respect and protection, but as public nuisances, to be disposed of like garbage. Scoular and O'Neill (2007) cite Zatz (1997) and lay some blame for this with policy makers who interpret whore stigma and violence as being grounded in sex work itself, instead of understanding that the social exclusion and victimisation of sex workers can be attributed to policies. Criminalisation and poor treatment of sex workers through punitive policies based on controlling individual behaviours and not systemic change perpetuates a framing of sex work involvement as marginal and not an industry within capitalism that our collective practices produce and perpetuate.

A logical reason why impoverished sex workers would be treated this way is if they are not really victims in our eyes at all. We must own up to this and stop lying to ourselves and each other about how sex workers are situated among populations who receive social protection. For victims, whom we do not deem complicit, we more fully invest in safety and support services, in their care and not their incarceration. For example, in the Irish context, SWAI fights for their rights and recognition and document the realities of the negative impact of legislation that criminalises their revenue streams. They are positioned in opposition to powerful religious factions, feminisms and the state. SWAI is well aware of the fact that some women's involvement in sex industries is due to the feminisation of poverty. According to the Central Statistics 2019,[7] Irish women took on the bulk of unpaid caring work, less than 12 per cent held executive roles, and they were at greater risk of poverty than men. Surely energies ought to be spent addressing structural inequities and not in indirectly criminalising poor women (and others) who trade sex. Many have died as a result of these kinds of policies. SWAI fights to end this kind of harm too and experience marginalisation as a result.

Class conflict

Class conflict hums in the background of debates about gender, sex and commerce. The poor and working classes are in a fight for scarce resources while facing domination, exploitation and extinction by powerful groups. Marx illuminated the struggle between capital (the bourgeoisie, petty bourgeoisie) and labour (the peasantry, the proletariat and the lumpenproletariat) and Weber examined bureaucracy and rationalisations to aid in understanding positionality, hegemonic power and the plight of those exploited, disenfranchised and disinherited. The 19th century, for example, was rife with colonial and capitalist exploitation as the European-led slave trade wound down mid-century, after 400 years and over 12.5 million souls were affected. There was rebellion from oppressed groups, including first-wave feminists, who fought for voting rights for some women. The 20th century was excessively violent and tumultuous as it saw both World Wars; the Cold War 1947–91; the Vietnam War 1955–75; the Civil Rights Movement 1954–68; and the second and third waves of feminism from the 1960s to 1990s. Genocides and holocausts were rampant in the 19th century and continued into the 20th. These included the Angolan Civil War that occurred intermittently between 1975 and 2002; the extermination of over 6 million European Jews and other racialised groups and sexual minorities from 1941 to 1945; the Cambodian Genocide 1975–79; the extermination of almost a million mostly Tutsi in the Rwandan genocide in 1994; the slow end to South African Apartheid from 1948 to 1994; and other atrocities such as the genocide in Darfur in 2003. Human history is wrought with conflict, hostilities and antagonisms between groups that involve both rational (all facts and outcomes weighed) and non-rational (no demonstrative weighing of facts) behaviours that are not easily resolved (Bartos and Wehr, 2002). Ultimately, antagonisms are a struggle for 'true interests' such as the fight for rights, recognition, dignity, access to resources (Bartos and Wehr, 2002) and, most notably, the elusive ideal of freedom. Living a dual life does not compare with these atrocities. I merely reference history in relation to class struggle and group conflicts between those with capital and those without, as the soil in the fields from which the fight for true interests persists. It is from this soil that sociological inquiry into inequity, power and division emerges. Debates about sex as work within and beyond feminisms are plants sowed in this field.

Divisions and debates about work, gender, sex, exploitation and liberation arise from deep-seated group conflict, in this case between men and women, and between privileged and marginalised women. I support the idea that 'the prostitute is a symbol of women's authority and a threat to patriarchy' (O'Neill, 2001, p 24) and add that sex workers are a threat to women who draw their tacit power and authority from combinations of oppressive power structures that include patriarchy, colonialism and capitalism. Patriarchy is a system that oppresses women, but not every woman because it exists in relation to other power structures. We cannot deny how some women benefit from the patriarchy, and with this power they influence sentiments about what is appropriate for other women and also for men who are less powerful than they are. Most obviously, a reductionist rendering of relationships between men and women, and sex and money, as purely exploitative leaves no room for consenting personal or commercial relations (O'Connell-Davidson, 1998) and no room for diversity of experience. From this perspective, commercial sex cannot be understood in the ways that contributors live it – as one of their jobs. Sex working and duality are methodologies that aid a struggle for resources in a ruthlessly classed, raced and gendered political economy.

Part II

The sample of contributors whose voices and experiences are reflected in this book comprise off-street, mostly online adult sex workers with experiences providing both contact (for example full service, massage and some commercialised role playing within Bondage, Discipline, Sadomasochism (BDSM)) and non-contact (webcam, pornography, phone/text sex, dance or modelling) services across sex industries. Most provided full-service sex industry work as independents or worked for escort agencies. All but three contributors moved from square work into duality. Their square jobs are categorised by sector to protect their identities.

Almost half of them worked in the private sector in for-profit businesses in retail, banking and the financial sector as well as entrepreneurs and consultants; eight (32 per cent) worked in the public sector in healthcare, education and justice; and four (16 per cent) held jobs in the voluntary/third sector, in a variety of NGOs and charities serving the UK and Europe. Their work experience in both square jobs and in sex work ranged from less than five years to more than 20. Several contributors worked multiple jobs in and out of sex work before entering duality. Some started their working life in sex work and then moved on to retail jobs and voluntary sector work. Others moved from sole square work to full-time education and then into duality. Several felt dissatisfied with square work, as one anonymous contributor explained:

> 'I got into sex work because I was disillusioned with [past square work] people would come with a problem and an issue or a complaint and the [professional role] is to help them like pursue that ... but 9 times out of 10 it's kind of a farce ... So what I observed is people would come in in pain and inner conflict and turmoil and we would get to the end of the [interaction] and that pain and conflict was just more deeply entrenched. There was no like ... healing or moving forward ... so I just grew totally disillusioned that I thought I want to work more therapeutically with people.'

Not all contributors entered duality from secure full-time employment. According to another anonymous contributor:

> 'It was only a 7-month contract and I wanted to get out of some debt and then I've actually had to leave my contract

job because my health was really bad, and the job made it worse basically … I live in a very expensive place. I thought right, I need to put a bit more effort into this [sex work] and then so I was on a couple of benefits but it was such a little bit of money … then that worsened at the end when I got one of my benefits taken off me and I was gonna be sanctioned for 6 months.'

Branwen (Full Service/Public Sector) describes her journey from challenging square jobs to duality:

'At 35 I left the [square job] because quite frankly everyday was like you have to be in form and getting up at 3am in the morning for years … I stopped it and then I got a new job. It was stressful and hard, and I've been spat at, I've been slapped, I've been sexually assaulted … then I started to get part-time work at [square job] because again I needed the money … then I went on the [website] not long ago because I had to start working for myself again in the sex industry.'

In terms of demographics, contributors are unremarkable. They were relatively diverse with respect to gender and sexual identity and age, with 16 identifying as cis-female and three were cis-males. A further three people were gender queer or fluid and four identified as femmes. The sample were a mixture of people who were heterosexual and 'straight for pay' and several who were lesbian, bisexual, gay and 'gay for pay', polyamorous, pansexual and queer. The predominantly heterosexual sample did not discuss any challenges or issues with their sexuality as it relates to duality, except for Zaine (Full Service, Massage/Voluntary Sector) who describes his gender and sexuality as being an asset in sex work. He believed that being gay supports his ability to be open about sex working, but poses a challenge in his square female-dominated work:

'I think being gay male it's a privilege to be out as a sex worker. It's really hard to find women who are out … but also I feel like it's problematic for [square job] … the majority of people who I work with are women. Like I don't engage with some because there is no point, they will dismiss what I say because I'm a male.'

Unlike contributors in Koken et al (2004) who were gay men who suffered stigma that forced them into a 'double closet', Zaine's white, gay, male identity supported him in being open about his duality to more people. Zaine discussed the intersection of a gay sexual identity, sex work and disease (Koken et al, 2004) within the context of symbolic stigma (Herek et al, 2005), but countered this with a recognition that being a white man shielded him from the harshest effects of whore stigma. Similarly, Mary (Full Service/Voluntary Sector) expressed that being a woman in SIWSQ was of great benefit. She believes that women have greater earning potential but also that women bear the strain of single parenthood and this complicates her duality: "I think being female it helps me with living a dual life … females get paid more and we tend to have more clients for example, but I do think that it's harder to be female and be a single mother particularly and live a dual life."

Contributors discuss having variability in how they present themselves to their different audiences and this flexibility in the presentation of self is at the core of successful duality. Most of the sample were between 31 and 40 years of age, with diverse outlooks on sex, work and longevity. Sierra (Full Service/Public Sector) constructed her interactions with older men as being 'commercial' whether she was involved in sex work or not:

> 'Any sex in a relationship is an exchange … You're 55, I'm much younger, and even if you didn't pay me and you were seeing someone like me there would be money involved … that's why women who look like me at my age are attracted to you … Even in our normal dating lives we are choosing people who have cultural capital.'

Sierra takes a Bourdieusian approach to relationships, viewing them as exchanges in capital and power.

Zaine felt that as a man in sex work he has a longer shelf life, but he still has to consider his age. June (Full Service/Private Sector) discusses her longevity:

> 'I'll do sex work for the next 10 years. My looks are my pension! … I'm amazed by the longevity of it. I really think you can make money for as long as you want to. "MILF" is the most searched for thing on the internet, like on porn sites and I noticed as well, on my ads I'm always putting like 37, 38 and cause I always thought you'll do better if you say you're in your 30s … but once I started putting 41, 42

on my profile my clients went up ... I get a lot of young guys ... and there are grannies working as well!'

Laith (Porn/Private Sector) started in adult film in his late 20s. As he ages, he is reassessing his comfort with being on screen with young women: "I'm over 50 now but I do not want to be on a set with some 20-year-old who thinks 'oh shit it's grandpa.'" Overall, age was a consideration but not a barrier to continued involvement in sex work, nor was race and culture.

Most contributors, 22, identified as white, with 11 being English, four Scottish and one Irish. Six contributors were white migrants from Europe, North America and elsewhere. There was one person of Persian descent and one of mixed heritage. Contributors talked about cultural diversity in sex work in ways that inform a UK 'whorearchy' elaborated on in Chapter 5; however, only a few contributors included race as an integral part of their identities or as influencing their abilities to construct and maintain duality. Joy (Webcam/Private Sector), a contributor who read my MA thesis, commented:

'I was reading your sex work exiting thesis, what I found interesting was the reference to you know, how do I perceive myself and the last bit I was reading was people's perceptions of themselves according to their race and I found that interesting because I've never ever, ever ever thought of my race as being part of my identity but then perhaps if you're from a racial minority, you would think race is more so part of your identity, that was interesting.'

Joy's understanding of race as being unimportant to her identity as a white woman may account for the virtual silence about this among most UK contributors. Class, however, had influenced Joy's approach to duality:

'Is class part of my identity? I would say yes ... I mean who I am and what I am, the type of food I eat and the type of books I read. What makes me successful in this? Well I never ever thought I would not be successful. Success is almost like an inevitability ... like a given, almost like a thread that runs through you ... In my regular job I never thought I wouldn't be successful ... In sex work, I went into it and almost like a mission ... I just simply treated it the same way.'

Joy's internalisation of structure, *Habitus* (Bourdieu and Wacquant, 1992) and practised way of being in the world, in addition to her disposition – tastes and preferences – all contributed to her approach to life, work and duality. Success was a given. Cleo (Full Service/ Private Sector) felt differently:

> 'I think even in my being out about it now ... there's a lot of race and class privilege that plays into my ability to do that ... like the class privilege and education and being able to sort of talk about things in a certain way ... I have very little baggage really, so I think that does give me like a certain ... like more freedom to be that fluid ... I think we all have to recognise that it is kind of contingent upon those privileges and contexts.'

Cleo attributes race and class privilege, particularly education, as elements that make her duality and ability to be 'out' possible.

Of the 24 individuals who provided information about their educational attainment, 16 held or were pursuing degrees: three BAs; seven MA/MScs; and six PhDs. These education levels are comparable to off-street sex worker samples in other research such as Koken (2012) and Sanders et al (2018). Contributors at times benefited from stereotypes about sex industry workers being impoverished, drug addicted and uneducated. These impressions about who trades sex support the concealment of duality. Stigma avoidance was prominent throughout their conversations. For example, Wyatt (Full Service, Massage/Public Sector) discusses his education as something that he used to confront stigma:

> 'What's interesting is the internalised stigma really prevents me from fully claiming the sex worker identity. I noticed when I first started doing sex work and I had my website I couldn't help myself but mention the fact that I had a [specialised advanced degree]. It took me about a year or so to realise that was bullshit, and I didn't need to, so I took that off the website.'

Although Wyatt decided to stop sharing his credentials on his sex work website,

> 'Sex workers do get this question from clients, like "is this your full-time job?" and it depends on my mood whether

I would give the right answer ... I was trying to ... I think, combat stigma before, because of recognition and worth and if you do sex work you're seen culturally, low, the lowest of the low. So, I wanted to like say "fuck you" ... I was feeding the stigma because I'm saying, I'm better than just sex work. I don't need to justify why I'm doing [sex work] or like qualify that by telling you I've got a degree.'

Sage (Full Service/Private Sector) challenged clients who perceived her as uneducated just because she is not originally from the UK:

'It's interesting because if you knock back clients they insult you by saying "you're [country of origin] and got no class" and I'm like "you're on the internet looking for sex at three o'clock on a Wednesday afternoon, let's talk about class" [laughter]. They assume that you're dumber because you're [country of origin] and then you have to remind them that you're onto your third university qualification, and then they say they have a bachelor's degree, and I say, "oh how quaint".'

Contributors often made social comparisons (Ashforth and Kreiner, 1999) that set themselves above other workers. If we treat educational attainment as cultural capital that is convertible to both economic and social capital (Bourdieu, 1986) we see that speaking about having an education helps avoid whore stigma in square communities where the assumption is that sex workers are not educated, but contributed to internalisation of stigma with sex work clients. Many sex industry workers are students. Sanders and Hardy (2013) surveyed 197 dancers in Nevada and the North of England and they found that 50 per cent were students who worked in the industry to finance rising costs associated with their education. Consequently, Teela Sanders of Leicester University launched a national co-ordination group on student sex work in 2019 that comprises sex workers, practitioners from groups such as NUM, and researchers to develop a toolkit[8] for staff of higher education to better support student sex workers.

Education, status frustration and emotional labour

Contributors who worked in higher education felt particularly betrayed because after long years earning degrees, they found themselves in unstable, low-paying term employment and in pointless administrative jobs in institutions that held little meaning for them. David Graeber calls this the 'bullshitization of academic life'.[9] This concept is explained in more detail in his 2018 book *Bullshit Jobs*. One anonymous contributor felt that their mainstream academic environment was exploitive: "It's very toxic like fucking [square job] it's so bad for relationships and bad for people and it's so exploitative, much more exploitative than sex work … and you never get paid for your work and never have job security."

Contributors in this sample are not alone in their struggle to survive even in academic careers. Several academics, who hold roles in public trust yet are poor, homeless or under-housed, do sex work.[10] Some contributors felt humiliated to take on low-paid menial jobs if they held university degrees and resented being forced to engage in the emotional labour of 'impression management' (Goffman, 1959). Emotional labour has appeared in literature related to quality of work experiences that are classed and gendered (Taylor and Tyler, 2000). Impressions are managed through direct behaviour through 'surface acting' (Hochschild, 1979) and through feelings and subsequent expressions of emotion work called 'deep acting'. Hochschild asserts that we are most aware of emotion work when our feelings do not match our performances. Contributors invest in performing the right show in front of the right audience, suppressing deeper feelings and monitoring their behaviour. Blaze (Full Service/Public Sector) explains:

> 'When I'm in the [public sector] job I have to put on an act and I have to pretend that I'm interested in things that I'm not particularly interested in or I have to do stupid [tasks specific to job] that are really dull but I have to get through it … And I have to do that in sex work as well … It's not always intimate. I mean it's like with anything else, you have sex with a long-term partner and sometimes it's intimate and sometimes it's like "oh for God sake, just get it over with I don't care" [laughter]!'

Sex as security

Selling sex as a side hustle may become more mainstream if working and middle class career employment and liveable waged jobs continue to dwindle. Precarity has crept into the formerly well-paid jobs in the public, private and third sectors, of which these contributors, based on demographics, would have had their pick. Precarity is a process that erodes through the introduction of short-term contracts and 'boom and bust' client-driven marketplaces:

It is not only 'the precariat' that has to deal with increasing precarity. Instead it is imperative to recognise precarity as an inherent condition of producers with capitalism on the one hand, while on the other also demanding more nuance in identifying the different processes through which precarity may increase across a diverse range of employment contexts. (Alberti, et al, 2018, p 450)

Those living dual lives aid our understandings of the labour markets and compel policy makers, carceral feminists, neo-prohibitionist crusaders and others of this ilk to take a closer look at our political economy, the work that is available and how adults may choose to define their employment within it. Our current context is one in which employed, working and middle class educated individuals engage in duality to address financial emergencies, to fund projects, such as tuition and mortgages, or as long-term financial strategies that facilitate social mobility. They define their toiling in both markets as work. Contributors are the *Precariat* who are involved in the process of 'precarisation' (Standing, 2016; Alberti et al, 2018), specifically, 'of living in the present, without a secure identity or sense of development achieved through work and lifestyle' (Standing, 2016, p 19). Being over-qualified and under-employed led to feelings of betrayal and exploitation, and many no doubt suffer from 'self-estrangement' (Marx, 1844) but this is the kind of desperation that our form of capitalism needs. Contributors then reconcile class conflicts, antagonisms, wealth disparity and precarious labour markets through duality and some achieve a desired class mobility.

Transferable skills

Alongside this, contributors spoke about the extensive skills that were marketable in both sex industry work and square work. Lynn (Full Service, Massage/Private Sector) states:

'I have an undergraduate degree in [omitted] which people think is kind of a fluffy degree but it taught me how to make written arguments and a lot of what I do at [square job] is written arguments ... if I'm writing an advert in sex work, which is so segmented by like class, so I play up the ways in which I am middle-class and educated and clients love to hear that you are at university.'

Helen (Webcam/Private Sector) applies her financial management and analytical skills from her square job to sex work:

> 'I think the skill of analysing data is surprisingly quite relevant to sex work. I'm able to tell you how much money I did in a month's time because I've got my spread sheet out in front of me and it's got all of my takings and costs and profits and so on. I can immediately tell you what my best days are for bookings. I go through and I note down the numbers of phone calls that I have, at what times of the day, and what days of the week, and then I'll track that to external events like while the football's been on, you know.'

Several contributors possessed this kind of business acumen. These practices of analysing client behaviour to ensure strategic involvement in sex work was common among this sample of individuals with high levels of educational capital. Helen explains further:

> 'I've got that advantage that I'm coming into the business already knowing a lot about how business works and already having worked myself and been self-employed ... If you don't know where the money's coming from and you don't know when the most profitable times or where the most profitable places are you might as well just hang up your bra and go home because you're leaving money on the table constantly!'

Helen reflects upon the stereotypes that sex workers are faced with:

> 'It's condescending attitudes and it's like "who would do sex work unless they had to?" and "if you do sex work that means you don't have any other skills and that's the only reason you would go into sex work" you know. "You must have failed all of your exams", and "you're too stupid to get a job shelf stacking", you big muppet! Like bitch please!'

Several contributors discussed having honed interpersonal skills that benefit them in work as well as their personal lives. Mary utilises hers:

> 'I get on good with people and I can make people feel comfortable very quickly ... but I mean like definitely like when a lot of clients are nervous, like they're only going to

be here for an hour so you've got 15 minutes to get them to feel comfortable enough to get all their clothes off, have sex and cum ... To get somebody to be that comfortable with you ... there's a lot of skills that you use in sex work that I do think that also help me in my square job as well ... facilitating people's ideas, listening to people, meeting people and yeah being like empathising with people, I think these help in both jobs.'

Juno (Full Service/Public Sector) is a licensed professional who discusses how skills earned in sex work improved her square work:

'As an escort I learned a lot of skills of not reacting and having a straight face and not laughing ... these skills I take into my [profession] that I got from escorting. I really have fun conversations with people. I don't feel uncomfortable about sex and things anymore as a [square job]. I mean when I was 18 it was like "oh my God I'm washing a penis", Now I'm like I could give a crap you know what I mean, I could be talking about the weather. It's the same skills that I learn as [professional] and I can take that into escorting.'

Juno continues:

'I went into escorting kind of after I started training to be a [profession] and I was quite shy and meek and when I went into escorting, I quickly realised that I had a lot of confidence to not be walked all over ... And God my confidence grew! ... it was seen in my grades, my first- and second-year grades are totally different. I got that confidence to say you know what, this is how it is, this is what we're going to do now ... take it or leave it, [laughter]!'

Too smart, too savvy

Joy feels that she brought skills from her private sector roles into sex work:

'Most of my skills in sex work I brought into sex work rather than them derived from being a sex worker. But I think now ... I'm much more aware of men and their bullshit, [laughter] ... where before I would just take them from, based on face value, and now I think that I've become very aware of when they are being genuine and sincere and when they're not just … from having encountered thousands and thousands of men.'

Having skills that are commutable across sex work and square work is not always beneficial. Mary explains:

'I have a research background and policy and working in a global organisation. I think my formal academic training tends to help with that. With doing sex work, in a way doesn't help knowing so much about the topic. Cause sometimes you want to just work and forget about everything and just you know go back to the bare bones of just having sex with somebody and then leaving but … it's almost like you think about it too much … and I'm thinking like my God I can't wait to write a paper on this.'

Juno also struggles to keep her professional skills at bay when she is doing sex work:

'Oh my God, you should see me! I try and turn it into some sexy thing and I'm like checking to see if he hasn't got something hanging out of the end of his fucking dick first [laughter] … and like so many times I'm like "oh you've got a skin infection" or something and the guy would be like "how do you know that?" I had a client a few years ago who had a sun burn and I'm like "right, what you need to do for this is …" and the client said, "I didn't realise that I was going to the GP!"'

Mary copes with her analytical thinking seeping in during sessions with sex work clients by shutting down intellectually:

'When I do sex work I need to turn off the critical thinking part of my personality. Like I think I've got two sides to me: I'm very bubbly … But then in my straight job I think I kind of do the opposite too and turn down the bubbly part of me and be more kind of studious and I want to be able to speak in a way that people recognise that I'm intelligent and I think that I'm one of them.'

There are more challenges to living a dual life that will be shared under a range of themes throughout this book. What runs through the experiences of contributors is a sense of loss due to the deleterious effects of stigma and the sacrifices that they have to make to achieve an average standard of living. Duality, moonlighting, side hustles are not new to the working poor and working classes and are embedded within a larger fight for scarce resources. Some feminisms, anti-sex politics and faith-based conservative ideologies have agendas towards ending the sale of sex through enforcement and displacement. These are myopic tactics that bring harm to the poorest sex workers who cannot work out of sight and shield themselves from stern gazes and stiff upper lips. Even sex workers who follow the law and work in isolation off-street find it difficult to avoid 'welfare visits' by police and investigative 'journalism'.

The layout and chapters

In the chapters ahead we gain a greater understanding of who is trading sex around us and why they do it, along with some of the challenges and insights they have to offer across a range of themes prominent in the social sciences and beyond. In Chapter 1 sex work 'exiting' literature is reviewed briefly to situate duality and this book within the context of that literature. This is followed by an explication of the labour market and the reasons why people trade sex, and ends with a presentation of information related to typologies and the Continuum of SIWSQ Involvement. Chapter 2 offers a deeper look into how duality is done through a review of role transition literature, and the experiences of contributors who move through various environments and construct the field and identity along the way. Chapter 3 shares more about duality and movement, audience segregation and how information communications technologies (ICTs) influence the concealment of stigma, work and relationships across sex work and square work and personal lives. The Dual-life Relational Paradigm illustrates the management of identity, audiences and information. In Chapter 4 commentary about the geopolitics of Brexit and how leaving the European Union (EU) may affect jobs in both sex work and square work is discussed. Contributors' experiences during the 2016 EU referendum 'visibilised' a UK whorearchy that privileges white Britishness in a social climate rife with nationalist rhetoric and anti-European/anti-immigrant sentiment. This UK whorearchy is portrayed as a stacking bookshelf, where various titles symbolise themes in mainstream societies that are constitutive of race hierarchies within sex industries.

Chapter 5 shares some of the challenges to living dual lives such as experiences of being outed, the weight of secrets and costs associated with having to lie about what one does for a living. Chapter 6 delivers more insights and experiences about precarity, alienation and how duality brings about 'flexicurity' for those who dare. The chapter presents an argument for an end to sex worker-exclusionary radical feminism (Miano, 2017) as part of the policy environment because unless there are drastic changes to how we *do* capitalism, sex as a side hustle and duality appears to be here to stay. Examples of how we treat sex workers who hold roles in the public trust are used to further illustrate the hypocrisy of the current 'sex worker as victim' narrative. Chapter 7 summarises the core themes touched upon in the book. It contains a bit of a rant and a call to action that will tie up some loose ends but will leave strands dangling for sex workers and interdisciplinary scholars to discuss and investigate in ways that are beyond my expertise and capacity.

1

"You can't make a living doing porn": Laith

Although this book is not about how people leave sex industries and instead how they maintain employment relations between the sex industry and mainstream markets, a brief review of 'exit' research is warranted. This will highlight some of the factors identified among mostly street-based sex workers and will problematise in/out binary frameworks as embodied by contributors to this book. This will be followed by a fuller exploration of sex working within and alongside mainstream precarious labour markets. In doing so I highlight motivations for duality as the drivers that influence and orient us all in our approaches to work in markets that are increasingly shaped by corporate interests. This chapter will end with a presentation of the Continuum of SIWSQ Involvement as a framework to understand (sex) work and transition and to situate duality within our culture of capitalism.

In or out?

Much of the literature on 'exiting' is based in role transition theory and cites former nun Helen Rose Fuchs Ebaugh (1988) who theorised a staged process of change where people change careers, move from contemplation and exploration to planning and execution, but never fully let go of elements of former roles because they may struggle with eliminating residual social labels. Several past studies on sex working populations (Potterat et al, 1998; Månsson and Hedin, 1999; Hedin and Månsson, 2004; Dalla, 2006; Sanders, 2007; Mcnaughton and Sanders, 2007; Baker et al, 2010; O'Neill et al, 2010; Matthews et al, 2014) interpret sex work as harm and as exploitation such that a failure to leave is hinged to personal characteristics or a combination of will and access to resources, as well as many structural issues. Factors that influence one's ability to leave sex work include: money woes; drug addiction; holding a criminal record; age; violence; type of sex work; location of sex work; the length of time involved in the industry; health issues; pregnancy; challenges with managing internalised stigma; motivation; frustrations dealing with clients; and the existence of or lack of supportive relationships, to name a few. Some researchers note that sex workers have incomplete role transitions because they fail to let go of aspects of sex work while moving on to more 'acceptable' labour and highlight the need for supportive relationships and therapeutic interventions to heal from childhood trauma and subsequent sex work involvement (Månsson and Hedin, 1999; Hedin and Månsson, 2004; Baker et al, 2010). The sex workers' desire to fully participate in diversion and exit programmes is also noted in subtext to the effect that sex workers are service resistant, thus troublesome or deviant.

Early studies of sex work exiting such as Månsson and Hedin (1999), upon which 'exiting' policy is based, excluded off-street workers and characterised their work or sex workers themselves as harm. There are contemporary studies that also do this (see Matthews, Easton, Young and Bindel, 2014). Some 'exit' literature posits transition as 'dangling between two life patterns, living in a state of uncertainty and ambivalence' (Hedin and Månsson 2004, p 225); 'yo-yoing' in and out of sex industry work (Sanders, 2007) and being unable to achieve sustainable incomes in either field. These studies document the transition out of the sex industry as challenging and uncertain, which is true for many, but not all. As these studies are among impoverished street-based workers, Sanders (2007) and Månsson and Hedin (2004) being the exception, they deliver part of the story needed to understand the plight of sex workers and contributors to this book. Scoular and O'Neill (2007) in fact critique Månsson and Hedin (1999) as it focuses on how sex workers are entrapped in prostitution; however, there was much diversity among their sample of women (n=25) who transitioned. One third easily moved from sex work to square jobs and education; one third stayed in treatment and the rest remained unemployed, yet emphasis was put on the 'social death' of women who did not exit (Scoular and O'Neill, 2007).

The term 'exit' itself is contentious because of its association with perspectives that view selling sex as inherently violent, requiring the immediate rescue of those involved. Leaving roles in sex industries for mainstream work is utterly complex and involves moving between (stigmatised) identities and activities to earn money that include but are not limited to exploitative jobs. I adopt the term 'transitioning' because it more accurately describes the actor-centred process of change undertaken by those who actively traverse difficult social relations and barriers to arrive at a level of involvement in sex work and square work that is manageable and meaningful to them. Transitioning, shaped mainly by the experiences of street-based workers, is skewed because these workers are seen by some as undeserving, nefarious and problematic populations in need of management and containment. The challenges they face are conveniently individualised.

For example, Hester and Westmarland (2004) developed a model of 'needs and support' (p 135) for street sex workers, based in how they have framed transitioning, as a staged process from 'Vulnerability' to 'Chaos' then 'Stabilisation' and finally 'Moving On'. Their model informs government policy, offers benefits and interventions from social services as 'stabilising' alternatives to sex working, in addition to housing, childcare and peer support. This support model is based on narrow assumptions about who trades sex and would be inadequate to support contributors to this research who want to leave sex industries. Contributors would be required to move from the earning levels noted herein, to abject poverty on government assistance. They would be further required to create dependencies and tolerate the hardships of stigma in their personal lives, due to government intervention being overtly linked to their sex working. Being known to multi-agencies and the state as a sex worker limits future possibilities. These things combined are in fact a recipe for social death.

Sanders (2007) argues that criminalisation, stigma and the denial of the legitimacy of sex work contributes to the marginalised status of sex workers and their inabilities to find and hold on to employment outside of sex industries. Scoular and O'Neill (2007) document the 2006 Coordinated Prostitution Strategy (ACPS), which marked changes in government approaches in the management of sex work in the UK. There was a shift from enforcement strategies to multi-agency regulation as part of progressive government, which they argue as being quite oppressive. Scoular and O'Neill assert that through neoliberal strategies, street sex work was associated with anti-social behaviour and that supports to transition were grounded in a 'linear victim to be saved by a process of responsibilization and individual change' (Scoular and O'Neill, 2007, p 766). They reference Walkowitz (1980) to highlight the lack of progress in this initiative as it was 'reminiscent of the Victorian era's focus on saving "Magdalenes" that led to the increased social control of poor women as a result of efforts and campaigns to save them' (Scoular and O'Neill, 2007, p 766). It follows that research, especially state-commissioned studies, will frame sex work as binary (in or out) and its continuation as problematic and stemming from personal and behavioural factors. For example, a participant, Kirsty, who was struggling with transition was described as one who 'flitted in and out of the sex work scene because of loneliness' (Mcnaughton and Sanders, 2007, p 895).

Research that highlights personal factors is important in humanising sex workers, sharing lived experiences and privileging their voices. Equal attention is needed so as not to side-step a full accounting of the forces operating within the field of trans-action in which this 'flitting' occurs. Law (2013), who conducted research among off-street industry workers, argues that situating sex industries as something to escape 'overshadow[s] the diverse labour arrangements and experiences of sex workers' (p 101). Brents et al (2010) highlight that some feminists hold two narratives for entry into sex work, one where innocent women are forced in and another where women choose; however, entry is correlated with the dynamics of the global economy, demographics and migration. In this respect, in or out of sex work is an inadequate framing as it ignores the fluidity and the changing contexts and conditions that influence decisions about work itself over the life course. Nor does it leave room for changes in definition, new or re-engineered ways of exchanging intimacies, like sugaring, and innovations such as duality, which as we saw in the Dollymop section, is not at all 'new' among poor and working class women.

Why trade sex?

The English Collective of Prostitutes' (ECP) report entitled *What's a Nice Girl Like You Doing in a Job Like This?* details challenges women face in work, comparing sex work and other jobs alongside the unpaid work they do at home. They discuss wages and take-home pay along with working contexts for women, finding that sex work brought in more money in less time (ECP, 2019). One ECP member explains best why sex is traded: 'We can stay in bed, live in squalor, we can live on bread and jam, but myself personally I feel I deserve more and so does my daughter. I choose to go on the street and earn that money because I want a better life' (ECP, 2019, p 29). Impoverished people trade sex for money when there are limited options to earn a living. Labour market conditions may change over time, but this essential fact remains. The majority of contributors here are women, who statistically obtain lower-waged, part-time employment, prone to precarity. Women have the added burden of disproportionate responsibility for the family and care for children, aging parents and other relatives. For the most part, contributors felt trapped in sole square work (and sole sex work for the few who had this work experience). Feminists who argue that women's bodies are commodified through sex work, such as those organising for the end of buying sex, in groups such as SPACE International[1] must shift focus to eliminating structural inequities such as poverty, because from the perspective of some sex workers, these radical anti-sex work feminists are embedded in, resourced by, and speak for the same hegemonic power structures that construct inequalities in the first place. Survivors of prostitution and survival sex tell horrific stories of abuse and harm that ought to move us all to action; however, their experiences occurred within the very criminalised contexts that many of us would like to see eliminated.

Full criminalisation of sex workers as seen in the US and de facto criminalisation in Ireland, Canada and the UK, for example, yield fines, imprisonment, diversion programmes, displacement, child apprehensions and, for some, deportation. It is not a surprise that active and former sex workers, as well as those who identify as survivors, had negative experiences in sex industries in these contexts. We frame sex workers as a public nuisance, enemies of feminisms and a scourge on civilisation, thus putting their safety in peril. Some vilify the poor and treat them as underachieving work dodgers. We cannot expect positive stories from sex workers in contexts designed to produce negative experiences and fear. Currently, radical feminists are instrumentalised by the state and instead of supporting sex workers and women in identifying and organising against the ways they are oppressed, which would be the feminist approach. Some feminists infantilise and pathologise sex workers, thereby reinforcing whore stigma and the subjugation of women.

Our labour market fully embraces short-term employment and low-wage/no-benefits jobs that provide little economic security and predictability, also known as precarious work. The term *précarité* was coined by Bourdieu and represents the distinction between casual workers and permanent workers (Alberti et al, 2018). Vulnerable workers are defined as those with low skills who may be susceptible to other discrimination in the labour market, such as gender bias; they may have family obligations and are likely to have no access to unions or labour standards and protections (Chaykowski, 2005). A 2012 report commissioned by the EU to examine precarious labour across 12 member states (UK, France, Germany, Bulgaria, Ireland, Greece, Italy, Latvia, the Netherlands, Poland, Spain and Sweden) found that those in insecure work are often excluded from other social supports such as housing, health care, pension and education (McKay et al, 2012). Mckay et al (2012) discuss labour casualisation and precarity as a combination of factors: 'including immigration status, employment status, temporal uncertainty, inadequacy of income and lack of voice over terms and conditions' (2012, p 107). These authors found that 30 per cent of all paid jobs in these EU member states (1987–2007) were precarious; 61 per cent of employees worked these jobs due to lack of choice; and false or 'bogus' self-employment (when companies force employees to declare self-employment but remain solely reliant on those companies for clients) and zero-hours contracts were among the worst types of exploitation that occurs (McKay et al, 2012). Pitcher (2015) found bogus self-employment in off-street sex industries and called it 'dependent self-employment' (p 114) where the self-employed are beholden to managers and third parties.

The current marketplace is conceptualised as being a dual labour market but there is little consensus on definition. Although this implies a binary that is beyond the scope of this book to fully investigate, some describe it the way Bentolila et al (2019) do, as the divide between open-ended contracts (held by regular employees) with fixed-term contracts (offered to temporary workers), a trend that began in the 1980s. Companies that operate in countries that offer little protection for employees will prefer fixed-term contracts, thereby casualising the labour market, because is it cheaper to fire these kinds of workers as they have little to no entitlement to severance or redundancy pay. This contracting reshapes the EU labour market, orienting workers towards side hustles, less stable working arrangements and iterations of 'self-employment' in our neoliberal contexts. Precarious work conditions extend to jobs requiring higher skills such as university lecturers and pilots, who suffer from term employment and income insecurity. For example, the average hourly pay for permanent workers in 2013 was £13.30 compared with £8.46 for zero-hours contract workers (TUC, 2015). Dual labour markets can also be conceptualised as primary and secondary markets, comprising core firms that shift risk to peripheral markets (Ghilarducci and Lee, 2005) but ultimately express deep and predictable class, race and gender divides between who has career employment and liveable wages and who is underpaid in insecure work. In every category of employment, from permanent to temporary, zero-hours and agency work, women have been paid between £32 and £61 per week less than men (TUC, 2015). Studies found that in the US white men with least education were paid more than other groups. Educated white men made more money than any other group; black women with college degrees earned the same as white men with high school diplomas (Ghilarducci and Lee, 2005).

Over two decades ago, Scambler and Scambler (1997) discussed material hardships and the de-standardisation of labour in the UK under Prime Minister Margaret Thatcher as a contributing factor to participating in sex work as resistance to (the feminisation of) poverty. Off-street workers they spoke with stated that they can make in two hours what most people make in 40 (Scambler and Scambler, 1997). O'Neill adds:

> Materially, [sex work] is often a response to poverty, financial hardship and need. We need to be aware of changes in the benefit system, changes in the care system ... council tax, recession and high interest rates ... we cannot look at [sex work] without looking at the social and economic contexts which give rise to it. (O'Neill in Scambler and Scambler, 1997, pp 11–12)

Sex workers and contributors here rationalise sex working through time/money returns on their energy investments.

Labour precarity is capitalists' way of saving on costs and externalising their responsibilities for labour rights and conditions. Some argue that short-term employment promotes flexibility and is beneficial to workers who are engaged in other activities, for example students; but how do they then explain student sex work? McKay et al (2012) see 'flexicurity' (the offer of employment flexibility and security) as an option to reduce issues inherent in labour precarity, which includes setting aside social security funds for temporary workers to access support and training during periods of bust and between hustles. Unfortunately, governments do not invest in this flexicurity model and refuse to provide these essential supports to workers and in this way provide the impetus for duality. Several sex work researchers suggest that labour policies, dwindling social supports and diminishing economic opportunities may push individuals towards sex work and away from insecure low-paying jobs (O'Neill, 2007; Bruckert and Hannem, 2013; Brooks-Gordon et al, 2015; Sanders et al, 2016; Pitcher, 2018; Sanders et al, 2018). Unfortunately, the implementation of various fee structures; commissions; oppressive practices of fining and obligatory tipping; or termination without notice occurs in sex industries too (Cruz et al, 2017).

Men in sex work also suffer from precarity due to how the markets have changed. Laith explains:

> 'Guys don't make a living in this industry. They make part time extra cash. They used to be able to make a living back in the 90s to early 2000 but once the [named a company] sites came out and crucified all of the large producers, the budgets got sliced and the guys basically got the short end of that.'

Men, in a study of self-employment among sex workers also commented on the limited employment opportunities for men in sex work (Pitcher, 2015). According to Laith, women must also diversify revenue streams to make a good living in the sex industry: "*You can't make a living doing porn.* You've got four revenue streams: porn; camming; making and filming your own content; and escorting. If you leave out escorting, you need to do the other three."

Duality can be understood as 'innovation'. Sex work is instrumentalised and a response and resistance to the vulnerabilities imposed by a precarisation of sex industries. Contributors improved their odds of financial security when they took advantage of *all* work available to them (albeit precarious) in both sex work and square work. They indeed found this 'flexicurity' through blending undesirable work arrangements in ways most advantageous.

The SIWSQ Involvement

The ways that contributors incorporated the work available to them across markets shaped the construction of a Continuum of SIWSQ Involvement. In addition to the lived experiences of contributors, three key typologies inform the development of the Continuum and they include Lucas (2005), Scambler (2007) and Pitcher (2018). Lucas categorised off-street sex workers into overlapping groups based on attitudes and motives, and on how much sex work they did. She includes those who were *casual* in their full-time sex working, only making enough to get by. There were those who were *instrumental*, who 'diligently' did sex work alongside other paid/unpaid jobs; and *savvy business women*, who professionalised their work over the long term. Contributors would be best placed where 'instrumental workers' and 'savvy businesswomen' overlap. Scambler (2007) developed a typology of six sex work career paths: the *Coerced*; the *Destined*, who have had sex workers in their families; *Survivors*, who are survival sex workers; *Workers*, who participate in sex work as a permanent job or career; *Opportunists*, who are more transient and intermittently involved; and finally *Bohemians*, who trade sex casually, as part of exploring sexuality unencumbered by financial need.

Finally, Pitcher's (2018) typologies are more recent and contain differing career patterns such as *interim pathways* among those who were instrumental about sex work, engaging for limited periods, to address needs and then transition out. Others were engaged in *multiple transitions*, moving across jobs in and out of the sex industry. They, at times, planned a return to sex work, or worked a *parallel pathway* (what

I term duality). Still others were in *longer-term careers* in sex work, in part due to abysmal work options (Pitcher, 2018).

It was important to capture whether contributors felt that they were more static in duality or moving towards sole sex work or square work. Incidental sex work (Morris, 2018) and involvement by those who do not identify as sex workers and have no premeditation or financial goals, along with survival workers, can fall within this continuum too and future research can explore this. People with no goals to earn money, Bohemians, and those who participate in sex work for survival are not represented among the current sample of contributors; however, I define survival work as a dynamic working condition that permeates sex work, square work and duality.

Contributors had various work histories and motivations for duality. Nineteen of the 25 (76 per cent) transitioned from full/part-time square, education or unemployment into duality. Several had been involved in sex work in the past. The remaining six (24 per cent) moved into duality from full-time sex work. Financial reasons for duality ranged from needing money to address *emergencies* or predictable shortfalls and cash flow issues that come at specific times of year. Six contributors (24 per cent) expressed participating in duality because living expenses and costs were higher before Christmas and when people were expected to pay for tuition and school uniforms, for example. Other emergencies included supporting themselves while temporarily unemployed, sudden illness or having unexpected bills and debts coming due.

Eleven contributors (44 per cent) had *interim-length finite projects* (with an end date) such as paying off debt or tuition for themselves or their children; getting on the property ladder; and acquiring financial security (savings or investments). Some desired flexibility in their employment while dealing with longer-term health issues or wanted to be more available during the day to raise children. Finally, eight contributors (32 per cent) were engaged in duality as a *lifestyle* or for long-term financial stability that would continue into the foreseeable future. These latter contributors viewed duality as a means of social mobility, to break through and win the class struggle for resources. This is not to say that they did not take breaks from either kind of work in favour of the other, only that they were strategically opportunistic! For them and others in the sample, time investments are reliable, but not an absolute indicator of where one's practices would fall along the continuum. For example, someone who engages in duality as long-term financial strategy may only do sex work 25 per cent of the time, or someone who is merely dabbling in square work may spend over 75

Figure 1.1: The Continuum of SIWSQ Involvement

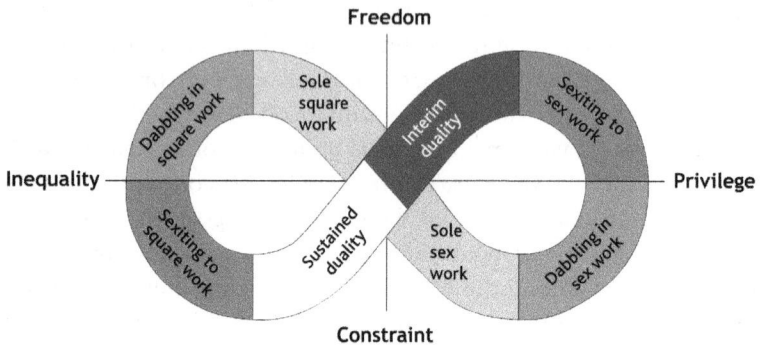

per cent of their working week doing these jobs. This nascent concept of duality can be expressed through three sets of practices:

- **Dabbling**: is a '*side hustle*' in sex work or in conventional work and doing so in less than 25 per cent of one's average work week. This is bidirectional and industrious. Unlike incidental sex workers, who may not acknowledge that they sell sex or identify as sex industry workers, or those who do not have financial goals (*Bohemians* to Scambler 2007), dabbling involves monetary motivation. Some contributors were disillusioned by sole sex work or doing square jobs alone and sought flexibility or to work less. Branwen's experiences (p 23) of having to wake early for a square job in which she was spat at and slapped is an example of this frustration with square work. Lucas's (2005) *casual workers*, who did little sex work, may characterise some contributors who dabbled. In this sample, dabblers tended to make up to £10,000 per annum in either sex work or square work.
- **Sexiting**: comprises behaviours associated with engaging in duality to transition to sole/full-time square work, or sole/full-time sex industry work. This 'transition hustle' expands my original conceptualisation (Bowen, 2013) that described 'sexiting' as sex working to leave sex industries. This is now expressed bi-directionally and acknowledges the reality that many engage in sex industries to escape square jobs. Many leave sex work through planned transitions that they fund themselves. Wedderburn et al (2011) documented that Jamaican sex workers left for nursing school and to run businesses. The *instrumental* group of contributors in Lucas (2005) may work this way as they also had specific financial goals to address. In this study Joy participated in duality to pay for her child's university education. Many individuals here have interim

projects and participate in duality between 25 and 50 per cent of their average working week or month. Several do sex work a few days a month or tour a few times a year. Engaging in duality for this purpose provides flexicurity (McKay et al, 2012) as contributors deal with gaps in income. For example, Cleo and Nova (Full Service/ Private Sector) went on tours during the year. They participated in sex work regularly and took on mainstream contracts, 'gigs' or other temporary employment as they sought stability and sole careers in one or the other industries. Sexiting contributors earned between £10,000 and £27,000 per year, combined income from duality.

- **Sustained Duality**: The key feature of engaging in duality for social mobility is that this sample showed no clear time investment or income range. Contributors worked either job seasonally, based on financial needs and changing goals, or to avoid debt and wage slavery. Scambler (2007) identified people who took on sex work as a career as *workers* and Lucas (2005) as *savvy businesswomen*. Both observers saw long-term sex work as a category of identity. Contributors in this study could professionalise their sex work but not accept it as their identity, in part as stigma avoidance and also because they draw esteem from university credentials and roles in square work. They transferred skills when it suited. For example, Helen analysed the market and strategically worked at times and in locations that would put her in front of her ideal clients. Juno used the interpersonal skills she attained in sex work to improve her square career. Contributors who committed to sustained duality earned combined incomes anywhere between £10,000 and £120,000 per annum.

The words that surround the Continuum of SIWSQ Involvement (Constraint-Freedom, Inequality-Privilege) symbolise tensions or what may be at stake within a given field and are up for discussion. These could easily be replaced with capitals in the Bourdieusian sense, or other values such as social status, cultural citizenship, integrity, and so on. Energies or forces are in play in all of our lives that constrain choice and reveal opportunities, and these are mediated by the various privileges and deprivations that exist. From a relational perspective, duality will be shaped by presentations of self (personal characteristics and the meaning they hold in your environment); who you know and importantly, who knows you (social capital); what they know (information management, selective disclosure, audience segregation); and how you are able to play your cards (performance, capitals, line and face) to attain your goals (income security, flexicurity, social mobility).

Figure 1.2: Duality project logo

Anti-sex work and neo-prohibitionist viewpoints of sex work being wholly and inherently harmful and oppressive, irrespective of how sex work and square work are (concurrently) lived, are weakened by the denial of other forms of work being more exploitative than sex work for some. This continuum is an attempt to illustrate duality as a choice architecture, where a range of working arrangements are possible given the environments, capitals and make-up of the fields where employment in sex work and square work coexist: the *matrix of possible events* that Goffman (1961) spoke of. It is also symbolic, as the eternity symbol embedded in the duality project logo portrays (Figure 1.2), that there is a constant calibration and re-harmonising that happens within and across these hustles, a fluidity that challenges binary understandings of sex work involvement by offering a more accurate picture of practices. The bidirectionality of *dabbling* and *sexiting* of side hustles and transition hustles is a novel way of conceptualising this fluidity. This advances analyses from sex work being at issue, to exploring the interrelationships people have with the availability of work itself, and how they construct their social worlds and working lives as a consequence. Duality is a blurring of dichotomies, a phenomenon that disrupts these neat categories of in or out and of 'exit', forcing discourse that may position sex working as better, equal to, or worse that non-sex work jobs, in addition to exposing skills transfer and the unique harms and opportunities experienced by those who work this way.

Duality emerges out of the political economy and is, in many ways, a form of resistance to oppressions, and a response to patriarchy and other systems of oppression that facilitate the concentration of wealth within only a few families. The inequitable distribution of resources, the control over how we can earn money and how much of it we are allowed to keep, affects the quality of life for the majority of the population. The Equality Trust's 2019 paper entitled 'Billionaire Britain'[2] states that the combined net worth of the richest five UK families is almost £40 billion of the country's financial capital, and the top 1 per cent own more than 80 per cent of the country's wealth. These kinds of statistics bring clarity to class struggle and to innovations such as duality. Although sex workers have been positioned by some as not belonging to our communities, 'theorised as part of the lumpenproletariat, prostitutes are social beings who by definition live outside of society, classified neither as workers nor as bourgeoisie, but always as Other' (Shah, 2009, p 5), these contributors are very economically active. They contribute the capital they earn in sex work back into the mainstream markets and vice versa. From their vantage points, there may be very little difference between labouring in sex industries and in square jobs as their need to do both is part of larger trends brought about by dual labour markets, devaluation and casualisation, and of divestment in paying the true costs of human labour, especially women's work.

Why duality?

Lynn, like most contributors, was motivated towards duality because she wanted to earn money fast:

> 'I got into full-service sex work because I wanted to make a large amount of money as quickly as I could and at the time ... I have friends who do BDSM and Dom and it requires so much planning and equipment and if you're just selling GFE or just sex, not even GFE, you don't need equipment. You don't need to be sending emails that are like a thousand words long of script for a role play. That's exhausting!'

Branwen wanted to maintain a lifestyle and own property but inflation and bills made this less possible without a second income:

> 'Yeah, I know full well I'm never going to get on the property ladder. Prices in this country are just stupid. So, I had to get back into [sex work] just to maintain a lifestyle and when I say a lifestyle I don't mean champagne or anything like that, I just mean being able to survive and have the nice things in life. Looking after a car, being happy to pay the rent not being you know, everything goes out to bills-wise on payday and then the next day after you're broke.'

The Office for National Statistics, for year ending 2017, found that the average household disposable income in the UK is £27,200[3] with an hourly living wage (beginning April 2019) of £8.21 per hour.[4] We collectively carry household debt in the amount of £1.23 trillion[5] (inclusive of mortgages, credit cards, loans, and so on); the top 10 per cent of households possess *five times* more wealth than the bottom 50 per cent of households. Furthermore, 41 per cent of people who hold a university degree are in debt.[6] Joy entered a dual life to ensure her child could go through university without debt:

'So, I decided literally overnight. I'd read some articles and as far as I'm aware I've never spoken to a sex worker about sex work and I decided, right, I'm going to need to find £20,000 in the next 9 weeks and how can I find that without borrowing additional money? ... I set about becoming a sex worker and that was I think 6 years ago.'

Likewise, Helen was looking to increase her income:

'I live in a really expensive area and I rent a tiny flat which even though I earn a pretty good salary, is all I can afford. So I was looking for ways to increase my earnings but it's ... the process of moving up within your existing career can be quite long and drawn out ... I enjoy my [square] job, I get well paid for what I do ... escorting, it's cash in hand, and there is a lot of money to be made. You know the first time I went to an out call and got paid 140 pounds for an hour of my time ... it was like more money in one hour than I've ever made in my life!'

For Helen and others, earning money in sex work was faster than the years it would take to advance in their careers. Joy explains her time/money rationale:

'I did a one-week tour of [UK] and I've come back with £7000 sterling. And I can't earn that in my normal professional job, bearing in mind I live in [omitted]. If I were working full-time pro rata it would be about £55,000 sterling per annum. My [sex work] however, which I'm very very very consistent with, I [sex work] all year-round income per annum is about £47,000.'

Joy's income from both roles is virtually on par but the time investment differs:

'I spend a lot more time in [sex work] than I do my mainstream job because as you know much of mainstream work we're not actually paid for. I may be contracted to do

32 hours per week but that 32 hours in reality is probably nearer 45 hours per week, and on top of that is my travel time. With [sex work] I can walk into my little dedicated spaces at 9pm in the evening and I can come out at midnight having earned £200.'

In a few days over a month, Cleo could earn her square monthly salary: "I'd see a client once a week or do like a few hours of [sex] work per week. In my square job, I was making my salary, something like £2000 a month ... I would easily make that in like a few days doing sex work."

Nova engages in sex industry work on contained days a few times a year. She attends various locations and sees clients and then moves on to her next location, after which, she returns to her home community and engages in her square job. She also refuses to work nights:

'When I'm in [city] I book a hotel for one night I make like somewhere around 2500 euro in 24 hours but that's only a few times a year. I ask for early check in around 10 or 11 and I make a booking for 2 hours and I charge 300 euro and then I break and book another client for an hour and then I break and maybe a dinner date. So, I always focus to get at least 1000 euro and I go to sleep around 11 or 12. I never work at night, and then the next day I might have one [client] at 9 o'clock until check out.'

Most contributors worked the way that Cleo does, seeing clients one or more times a week or a few times a month, supplemented by the tours that Nova describes. Alice (Full Service/Private Sector) earns a good living from duality and had this to say:

'The money is 70% sex work just because it's far better paid. I'm very fortunate because I have a reasonable pay in my salary before, earning about 75,000 pounds ... but if you were only working a minimum wage job well God sex work ... why wouldn't you do it [laughter].'

Duality clearly pays well and the combined revenue of the 24 contributors who told me about their earnings is documented in Table 1.1. The income cut off at £27,000 reflects the average national income around the time of interview, circa 2017. By way of comparison, 50 per cent of contributors (n=320) in Sanders et al's (2018) sample of

Table 1.1: Total combined income in SIWSQ

Income range	Number of contributors
Up to £10,000	2
£10,000 to £27,000	3
£27,001 to £50,000	10
£50,001 to £75,000	7
£75,001 to £120,000	3
Opted out	1
Total contributors	**25**

internet sex workers spent less than 10 hours per week in sex work, earning less than £20,000 per annum to supplement other incomes. This additional revenue makes all the difference for some. Notably, 20 contributors (83 per cent) made more than the national average income in 2017, with half of those almost doubling or tripling it.

In terms of time investments, almost half of the contributors (n=12) stated that they spent less than 25 per cent of their time doing sex work in any given week. With respect to square work, the picture was virtually reversed, with 12 contributors (48 per cent) spending over 75 per cent of their time in these jobs. The time/money rationale was problematised by the inclusion or omission of unpaid time in the form of downtime. This comprises time spent waiting for clients, in correspondence, preparation or travel, in 'relationship building', and in customer acquisition. Some valuable time also went to 'time wasters' who are potential customers but who never convert to paying customers. Only the entrepreneurs incorporated this unpaid time. Sierra processed this out loud:

> 'There is work that I don't recognise as work, like talking with idiots on the website when nothing happens in the end, and time wasters. So actually, it's less money [from sex work] than I believe. Then my feeling is like "oh I'm going to see that person and I have a lot of cash", and that makes me feel like "oh I got a lot" but actually if you count all of those hours talking to those guys, which end up not actually booking ... it would be like 30% of my total income I think.'

Of those who acknowledged this unpaid time, they either lamented it as time wasted or explained how they used this downtime to do other work. Joy explains: "There is quite a bit of hanging about and quite a bit of sitting about, you know, maybe in an apartment or a room … it does give the opportunity to do lots of other … exploring other avenues … researching something."

Blaze has plans to use her downtime in sex work while living at her working flat to do schoolwork:

> 'I would want to spend 3 full days doing sex work and then 2 days [schoolwork] and then every other weekend I'd be in the [square job] … Once I'm in the flat I can be in the flat 5 days and use it as an office and in between bookings. I can do [schoolwork] cause some days it's dead, you don't always make money.'

Sage explains the 'costs' of unpaid time in sex work:

> 'The problem with sex work is that there is so much unpaid work in terms of managing your schedule and there is no point saying that you charged £200 an hour because if you were being available for a client for 10 hours a day and you only get one client then it's 20 quid an hour. And plus, the e-mails that you respond to … so maybe it's £15 an hour … so about 40% of my time is taken up with sex work.'

Sage, like Joy, discusses boredom:

> 'I couldn't do sex work if I didn't have another job. It would just, it would just do my head in cause you get the same e-mails from clients and then I find it too boring actually. I think I'd be doing myself a disservice if I spent too much time on sex work.'

The sentiment 'whoring is boring' (Scambler and Scambler, 1997, p 114) holds true for several contributors and many are thankful that they have other work and school to fill their downtime. Some contributors, like those discussed by Dodsworth (2014), used the flexible working hours to raise children.

Duality brought freedom and money, a new experience for contributors who grew up poor. Lucas (2005) reports: "Over and over again, my interviewees emphasized wages and freedom as the primary attractions of prostitution" (p 523). Sage remarks: "I'd say it [duality] allows you to be freer … I grew up in poverty and that's no exaggeration and growing up without money in a difficult situation and then getting it teaches you what money actually means, and money means security, choice, freedom."

Duality for Zaine meant that he can focus on square work when he is not well enough for sex work:

> 'I have an STI and I'm going to all of these clinics and I'm trying to figure out what it is, and I can't see any clients, so it's great that I have square job because I know I'm going to have money at the end of the month. If I was doing only sex work that would be most stressful. You really rely on your body and your sex work and your sexual health and if you have something then you would be fucked for that month.'

For Juno, her public sector job is a reliable fallback: "My [square job] is stable and if sex work did dry up or when I get old and not very interested in it anymore then [square job] can kind of be a full-time career at that point." Kora (Full Service/Public Sector) talks about duality limiting burn out more generally:

> 'The benefit [of duality] is that you're not dependent on any one job. So, you can get the opportunity to be more varied and not be burned out by one thing. You can be burned out from working too much in general … it's like that for any other job, for all jobs.'

Helen explains the dangers of doing sole sex work: "If you're only escorting and not doing anything else I think there's a danger that you feel like the whole world is about sex work …" Helen adds:

> 'I think that's the big advantage that I've got as well as having that civvy job as a backup is that I don't ever feel that I have to take a booking. Whereas oh God, if I was thinking that I might not be able to pay the rent this month … I don't ever feel that I have to go ahead and take the booking because I need the money. I will always turn a customer down.'

The inability to refuse work – part of my definition of survival sex – through being forced, economically or otherwise, to trade sex is a situation that we must unite across the political and ideological spectrum to prevent.

In this chapter, exiting literature that shapes binary understandings of sex work involvement was used to situate the range of practices between the polarities of in or out. Contributors shared their experiences of concurrent sex work and square work, ensuring that they, although hidden, can no longer be invisibilised in 'exiting' or transitioning discourses. Furthermore, the inability to find stable work in or out of sex industries is not a character flaw or failing of deviant sex workers, but a social issue, influenced by class conflict, the behaviour of markets (that we all shape), and the choices and values of those in power. Discrimination, stigmatisation, and the exclusion of the working class (including sex workers) in setting priorities and resource distribution is evident in the current state of our markets and we all have the power to change this.

In the next chapter, role transition among contributors is presented to illuminate shifts in persona, identity and *habitus* necessary in the performance of roles in disparate working and personal fields of trans-action.

2

"I am the same me in bookings as I am out": Sage

The Continuum of SIWSQ Involvement provides a framework for situating contributors' working lives into distinct yet overlapping labour markets; however, contributors must engage in these diverse fields in ways expected of them while concealing the information about them detrimental to respective environments. The focus of this chapter is sharing the intricacies of moving between jobs for contributors and comprehending them through identity (re)formation as it relates to role transition and 'rituals of movement' (Ashforth et al, 2000). We will be touching on impression management and stigma avoidance as important elements involved in successful role transitions (these techniques will be discussed in more depth in Chapter 5). The chapter ends with commentary from contributors about managing duality and role transition while working from home.

Identifying with (sex) work

Several contributors identified with both jobs as expressions of who they are, and some resisted the idea that they ought to identify with work at all, and even challenged the line of questioning. Juno explains her feelings about both jobs:

> 'I enjoy my job as a [public sector professional] don't get me wrong but you have to be very square very boring you know, Angel Gabriel all the time ... Escorting, you know what I can be a little bit crazy and a little bit unconventional and wear some crazy clothes and it's fine and I like that ... I do like both of my jobs it's just unfortunate people won't accept that I can do both and be like a safe person as a [public sector professional] and as an escort.'

Joy does not identify with sex work:

'I identify the most with the real me which is my job as a [private sector professional] … in the beginning of sex work it felt almost surreal being this other person answering to a name that's not your own, so I don't actually identify with the sex work at all. I am a sex worker, but I've had very very little opportunity to talk to … or to engage with other sex workers other than on forums and websites like [omitted]. So, because I'm not, it's just something I do principally for the finance for the money, but I don't identify with, that must sound pretty bisarre.'

Franco (Full Service/Private Sector) also wrestles with how he identifies across fields of interaction:

'I read about your research and the duality … I launched my [square business] only a year ago and it basically wasn't working, and I was really confused, and I had a couple of clients and it didn't feel quite right. I felt like a fraud, you know, I'm a hooker and a [public sector professional] and I felt like I shouldn't really be doing both, because it's one or the other and in my head … The problem was that I only felt like myself when I was doing the escorting … I felt guilty … I actually think that that's a little bit of internalised whorephobia and I think that "oh I can't do [square job] because I'm an escort" and what I'm actually doing is delegitimising the sex work.'

Kora questioned being asked about identifying with sex work or square work as it presupposes that individuals identify with work, or in some way ought to:

'I approach it very politically and I can hardly detach from what I know it means if I say I identify with a job. And I am completely aware that it's absolutely fine to want to identify as a sex worker but I hate the fact that in neoliberalism we have to identify with our work … if you were to identify as a sex worker and taking it as your identity and not as a job you do, you risk reproducing the stigma on yourself, unless you are the one determining what it means to be a sex worker … maybe at some point it would have been as a sex worker but I'm scared of saying it.'

Doing sex work but not identifying as a sex worker may be stigma avoidance but it is also resistance to oppression. The power to define is an incredibly important personal and political project. In her 1982 speech at Harvard, Audrey Lorde famously stated:

'[A]s a Black lesbian mother in an interracial marriage, there was usually some part of me guaranteed to offend everybody's comfortable prejudices of who I should be. That is how I learned that if I didn't define myself for myself, I would be crunched into other people's fantasies for me and eaten alive.'

Fears associated with identifying as sex workers are not only related to sex, work and whore stigma but are part of the larger oppression of sex industry workers who lack the political power to self-define as a community and thus are defined by others. This is changing of course, as sex workers and allies claim space.

Duality is a deeply embodied experience. Sex work and square work are positioned as disparate markets, yet the trans-acting is done by one being, forced to schism in adaptation to two or more dynamic fields. The parallels between sex work and square work are lived through the core and peripheral features of roles in both marketplaces. Reminiscent of Rumi and Plato, Goffman expounds upon dualism and concealed stigma:

they *play both parts in the normal-deviant drama* … the individual may be able to perform both shows, exhibiting not only a general capacity to sustain both roles, but also the detailed learning and command necessary for currently executing the required role behavior … *stigmatized and normal are not merely complementary; they also exhibit some striking parallels and similarities.* (Goffman, 1963, p 133; emphasis added)

Theories of identity and becoming

Post-structural theories of identity such as those formulated by Stuart Hall help explain how the identities of those living dual lives can be (re)formed and situated in time and space. Beyond being fixed and stable, group-based or interactional, Hall's concept of cultural identities (Hall, 1994, 2011) ties its formation to history, norms and internalised structure as well as being in constant flux due to changing social dynamics, power and representation. Hall's work on identity was grounded in the Afro-Caribbean (and Asian) experiences of self and the diaspora of continuity and discontinuity that came about as a result of slavery, migration and transportation. He states that cultural identity 'is a matter of "becoming" as well as of "being"'; '... like everything that is historical, they undergo constant transformation ... far from being eternally fixed in some essentialised past, they are subject to the continuous "play" of history, culture and power' (1994, p 225). This conceptualisation of cultural identity means that identities are agential and responsive, and constantly in the process of being (re)produced. Hall suggests that we must think of identity 'as a "production", which is never complete, always in process, and always constituted within, not outside representation' (1994, p 222). Contributors are actively reinventing themselves in their disparate work environments and their personal lives. They are transitioning between work roles and *becoming* in the process.

Some contributors do not feel that they make any major adjustments to who they are as they move between sex work and square work. An anonymous contributor, who is a lifestyle submissive and open about that in her square work, required no mental preparation for moving between roles in administration and BDSM: "I've gone from [square] work and then straight to my Dom's house for pro-subbing, and I haven't really done anything physically or mentally to kind of switch gears. I don't know if just being a lifestyle submissive helps that."

Sage viewed her ability to perform both roles and keep hold of her concept of self as a skillset:

> '*I am the same me in bookings as I am out* ... it's the same role you step into in [square job] ... you become a hyper version of yourself and so many lies that you spin when you're in [square job] and you do it in sex work. It's actually a skill set about being charming and engaging, and disarming. Getting people to warm up to you.'

Other contributors had to mentally prepare for transitioning between roles, implement 'rituals of movement' and make some adjustments to their performances of self.

Managing stigmatised identities across disparate social environments has been explored by theorists such as W.E.B. Du Bois, Franz Fanon, Goffman and others. Contributors may develop what W.E.B. Du Bois (1903) called a 'double consciousness', a maladaptive strategy that causes mental conflicts in contexts where people cannot be wholly themselves and must in fact shield their thoughts, ideals and strivings. Du Bois examined the African and American identity formation and its management for black men in post-emancipation America, where these two identities are constructed as separate, with differing opportunities and life chances attached. He writes: 'One ever feels his twoness, – An America, A Negro [sic]; two souls, two thoughts, two unreconciled strivings; two warring ideals in one dark body, whose dogged strength alone keeps it from being torn asunder' (Du Bois, 1903, p 2). This double consciousness relates to Hochschild's (1979) concept of 'emotion work' of impression management. The Du Boisian approach to understanding duality resonates with contributors who, in working contexts, must always keep part of what they do veiled whether they identify as sex workers or not. Helen believes that she is skilled in mentally compartmentalising her world and being *who is required* in each situation due to her upbringing:

'I probably have learned to compartmentalise as a result of my upbringing. Our parents were quite weird, and I was a very different person at school than what I was at home, so in a way that's probably given me a grounding in how to be two different people. And how to kind of be a certain way with certain people and not with others.'

Viewing oneself through the eyes of others, Cooley's 'the looking glass self' (Mead, 1930), may be important for appearance management, to 'read the crowd' and adjust behaviours, but may cause injury to oppressed persons. Although the black experiences of two-ness that Du Bois is referencing are about a stigma that cannot be concealed unless individuals pass as white, the essence of a double consciousness is a true lived experience for contributors. Franz Fanon (1967), a decorated WWII soldier who won the *Croix du Guerre*, had a similar concept of a 'twoness' where American black people had to constantly view themselves through the eyes of an oppressor, who denied their citizenship and even their humanity (Moore, 2005). Although interactionists such as Mead (1929) argue that the self is only known indirectly through engagement with others, for oppressed populations this may be unhealthy. Moore suggests that 'it is not psychologically healthy to measure your worth though the eyes of others … to be denied full expression of your blackness or manhood in a white-dominated society' (Moore, 2005, p 753). Laith agrees. He feels that having different personas that one moves in and out of is unhealthy: "I am me whatever I'm doing … I've seen people [have different personas] and it's always struck me as unhealthy cause I've always felt that when people do that, one of them isn't real." Moore suggests that vacillating between being black and being American has fractured the psyches of generations and having to base an identity on another's construction of reality is unhealthy and disempowering. Mary questions how she is even able to manage two personas:

> 'I don't know if this is about internalised stigma or shame, but sometimes I ask the question how I can do it? Like why it's easy for me to flip in between roles? To put on different personalities, to put on different personas? … I know that one of my skills is that I'm a bit of a chameleon.'

The ability to become what is needed and perform acceptably in roles was documented in research among working class youth who went to university among the elite (Abrahams and Ingram, 2013). They had a *chameleon habitus* adapting their behaviours, switching between fields, internalising structure (which are people in interaction) and at times concealing markers that exposed them as being working class or posh, as the situation required. Mary identifies herself as a social chameleon and links her ability to adapt to roles in differing fields to internalised whore stigma:

> 'There's two sides to being [able to move between SIWSQ] and the other side is like if you do it so often. Like you need to make sure you have a grounding about who you are because otherwise you can add on all of these layers to your personality or switch your personalities so flippantly and easily … you just need to remember exactly who you are and what your foundations are. I think for me now having kids makes it a lot easier cause that's the most that you're ever yourself.'

Dodsworth (2014) discusses the challenges associated with managing dual identities of 'sex worker' and 'good mother' as the two roles are disassociated in the minds of the public. Contributors who did not identify as sex workers separated personal and social identities to play several roles that supported simultaneous sex work and motherhood. For Mary, motherhood was her core identity, which anchored her and guarded against losing her sense of self while managing duality. She believed that being a sex worker made her a better mother.

Remi (BDSM, Porn/Private Sector) explains how She uses wardrobe to manage identity:

'The only time I bother to put makeup on now as my personal self is if I'm going to like a bar. If I'm just going out for dinner, I won't put make-up on and I keep my clothes separate. I didn't for years because I was like "oh no, I wear stuff like both of my selves." I found myself compartmentalising, and my sex work persona has all of these old fashioned smart mumsy clothes like a teacher or an auntie would wear. Which I would never wear as my personal self. And when I'm being me, I wear a lot like ... hippie stuff and my sex work persona would never wear that ... My presentation is nicely compartmentalised in a way that serves me not feeling like I'm working all of the time and I feel like I'm keeping enough back. There's dress up possibilities and there's wardrobe possibilities which I never give to my sex work persona.'

Remi states that she is "keeping enough back" so that she maintains a core sense of self outside of sex work and her other jobs. This is *chameleon habitus* operationalised through attire.

Role transition

Role transition was discussed earlier as part of transitioning or 'exiting' from sex work and applies here again as part of moving between industry work and square jobs. Role transitioning is something we all do in everyday life, whether it be less frequent macro changes in career, or more regular micro level movement from work to roles at home. Ashforth et al (2000) define a role as a persona with associated values, norms and behaviours and these role identities are socially constructed self-definitions. Accordingly, there are *central features* that are essential to the role such as specific skills for example accounting, and *peripheral features* or qualities such as intelligence. These roles and personas exist along a continuum of integration (flexibility and broad applicability of features) and segmentation (highly specialised features with context-specific applicability) where the more segmented a role is the harder it will be to transition out of it or to it from other roles. The opposite is true for highly integrated roles (Ashforth et al, 2000). There exists a rare 'Jekyll and Hyde dualism' (Ashforth et al, 2000) with very highly segmented roles among those who keep their work lives concealed from their families. People who do sex work alongside mainstream jobs may have a mixture of integrative and segregated central and peripheral features to balance but because sex work is stigmatised, transitioning may feel like a Jekyll and Hyde dualism.

Macro role transitioning has been studied among religious converts, for example, who make radical changes to their systems of meaning-making or their *universe of discourses* (Snow and Machalek, 1983) and how they talk about themselves, their relationships and environments in the context of their new roles and beliefs. There are a series of principles of conversion and among them are *biographical reconstruction*, where old and new, past and present, are dissolved and (re)constituted. People essentially rewrite their biographies, let go of elements that no longer hold meaning and keep experiences that mark transformation and best reflect the new self. Therefore, some theorists suggest that role identification is hedonistic (Ashforth et al, 2000) as people will identify with the most socially valued roles. This identification may be influenced by culture contexts of collectivism vs. individualism; gender identification; the uptake of rules; and the amount of inequality tolerated in a society. Snow and Machalek draw on Mead (1932) to emphasise that biographies and identities are reconstructed through new experiences and this ties in with Hall and Du Gay's (1996) cultural identity as being manufactured within discourses and as a product of difference. Transition in the macro sense is an ongoing project of identification and culture. Contributors who move between sex work and square work are adjusting to working cultures and discourses; however, unlike conversion, their transitions are regular and bidirectional.

Macro role transition involves an *adaptation of a master attribution scheme* as part of conversion that helps individuals explain cause and effect in their lives. Their behaviours are attributed to internal (disposition) and external (environmental) causes. As part of macro transitioning, people utilise context-specific vocabularies that centre around one acceptable reason why things are the way that they are and then they organise their worlds of relations accordingly. For example, some contributors are motivated towards duality to exercise some degree of control over their working lives and income. They feel that they are circling the drain, drowning in debt, underpaid and over-qualified. Duality provides the flexicurity needed to avoid the exploitation of sole work across marketplaces. This is their master attribution scheme, their *raison de faire*. The time/money rationale for sex working and duality may also be associated here. Those who convert also demonstrate a *suspension of analogical reasoning* where there is only one truth, one way of understanding the world and an *embracement* of the convert/new role that governs frameworks and behaviour as people adapt to role expectations and trans-act accordingly.

Wacquant (1990) argues that role transition is beyond a staged process of change theorised by Ebaugh (1988), for example, and instead that roles are part of a broader social network of relations, and one's disposition or practised way of being in the world. It is tied to *habitus*, their internalisation of social structures (capitalism, patriarchy and colonialism) that form the cognitive categories through which they understand the world (Wacquant, 1990; Bourdieu and Wacquant, 1992). Simply put, role transition involves one's belief in the stakes and profits associated with role or career, and what transitions they believe are possible given their biographies and how internalised structures have manifested within them. People continuously conduct the 'ideological work' of matching the realities of their workaday lives with their cherished convictions. They utilise various 'capitals' (Wacquant, 1990; Bourdieu and Wacquant, 1992) – such as social relationships, information and financial assets – to maintain or change the roles and environments. As their fields of interaction change, contributors open themselves to new risks and new possibilities within dynamic contexts.

Rituals of movement

Regardless of scope (micro/macro), successful role transition requires the implementation of 'rituals of movement' (Ashforth et al, 2000) that facilitate the adaptation of role-appropriate core and peripheral features. Three types of rites of passage have been theorised by van Gennep (1960) that apply here: (a) rites of *separation*, which are cues that support role exit such as getting dressed, having a shower; (b) rites of *transition*, the mental preparations needed for switching cognitive frames and ways of thinking; and (c) rites of *incorporation* that involve a change of environment such as commuting which helps to bring closure to a prior role and prepare an individual for the next one (Ashforth et al, 2000). Some contributors spoke about these rites but did not adopt any. Cleo explains:

> 'I would be quite nervous before I saw a client and then kind of maybe a bit of like adrenalin or something but otherwise mentally … Not mentally … I didn't feel like there was a huge switch or a huge separation there in terms of my mental state … I mean I know people who have like more specific rituals for sort of changing from one into the other and I don't think I've ever really had that.'

Some contributors had to utilise rituals to transition. For some, adjusting to movement between sex work and square work was difficult initially but became easier over time. Alice explains:

'I found it quite difficult to start with in that I would be doing square work and just hacking away at my email and then my sex work phone would ring and then be [sex worker name], so it was a bit of a head fuck, but I can just do it now.'

Helen had a similar experience: "It's quite automatic now. The first few times I was kind of like 'oh god I'm being a sex worker now' [laughter], it was quite freaky ... I found it quite difficult ... I got used to that quite quickly and it's become quite easy."

Juno required some mental preparation to switch from her square job to sex work:

'I don't really take on the spot bookings unless I've got the day off, so if I went to do a shift at [square] work I would know about that booking before I go to work, so I've got it in my head that I'm going to do [square job] ... and then it's time for escorting, so I kind of have it in my mind which mentally gets me quite ready and thinking about it.'

To mentally switch away from sex work, June engaged in a rite of separation (Ashforth et al, 2000) by turning off her sex phone (device management as it relates to audience segregation will be discussed more fully in Chapter 3). She explains:

'Sometimes when I'm off I don't want to look at my phone and I don't want to answer messages, and then I'm like maybe I would do better if I would check my messages more regularly ... You know what would really improve my life is a secretary ... especially if a few of us shared someone and who could schedule us, it would be amazing.'

The Möbius strip

The Möbius strip analogy best illustrates role transitioning as described by contributors. This one-sided, one-edged strip was not named after its original discoverer, German mathematician Johann Listing, who created it in July 1858, but after astronomer and mathematician Ferdinand

Figure 2.1: Möbius strip

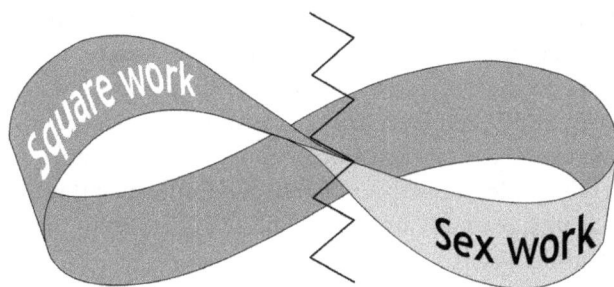

Möbius who developed the idea in September of that year (see Figure 2.1).[1] The idea is that if an ant were to traverse the surface there would be no noticeable demarcation from one side to the other. The ant would seamlessly and endlessly walk along both sides of the tape.

The Möbius strip depicts a balancing or harmonising of sex work and square work that must occur for duality to be a successful venture. Contributors moved between roles mentally, physically and spatially, establishing routinised role transitions. This is not to say that their practices were unchanged, just that they were able to maintain core self-concepts while 'becoming' in diverse work roles. Contributors discuss a sensory mental barrier that is surely erected due to whore stigma and role expectations, where contributors prepare for changing character and personas. This is highly related to Bourdieu's *habitus clivé* (Friedman, 2014), a splitting of embodied ways of being in the world to perform best in two distinct fields. The jagged line may be reminiscent of W.E.B. Du Bois' 'veil' or colour line that prevented white people from seeing black people as equals, and black people from understanding themselves outside of how white people constructed blackness. It is the bifurcation of oneness where workers living dual lives must police themselves through the eyes of square people or sex workers, depending on the environment and role they are enacting. It is the site of mental shifts and rites of passage such as showering, dressing, the scenting of environments, the moving into sex work-only spaces in their homes, and of course commuting. The jagged line may represent the pause before passing through the curtains (to evoke Goffman's 1959 dramaturgical analysis of the presentation of self) and entering the stage of either sex work or square work. Gloria Anzaldúa's (1987) poem *What does it mean to live in the Borderland?* expresses what living between two worlds is like. She argues that those who live at a border have no place of safety, are both at home and strangers. For Anzaldúa, these borders and their residents are liminal spaces where 'people walk through you', individuals living there become the battlefield itself ... both the embodiment and the location of conflict.

Through the reconciliation of sex work and square work, contributors work in the difference. They embody the antagonisms between precarity and income security; alienation and acceptance; respectability and taint; concealment and revelation; and of conformity and innovation. Their identities are emergent and (re)formed through the practice of duality, precisely what Hall and Du Gay (1996) meant when he said that identity is a product of difference.

Making space: working from home and role transition

Other rituals of movement were exercised among contributors who worked from home. Changing clothing, for example, and making alterations to home working environments was part of role transitioning and making mental shifts between personas. It may seem obvious that a sex worker would change clothes, particularly if we think of the stereotypical images in mainstream media of sex workers in high boots and miniskirts leaning into car windows under the hazing glow of a streetlight. Beyond just changing out of sensual attire and make-up, separations in clothing kept identities apart. Rain (Full Service, BDSM/ Private Sector) works from home and does not have to physically present herself to colleagues in her square job: "I do my square job from home ...I basically communicate over email and I don't have a lot of human interaction, so I don't really have that management of demeanor. I don't have to worry about censoring myself."

Remote working reduced appearance management activities, thus making the transition between jobs smoother. Contributors, however, made amendments to their homes that supported role transitions and 'twoness' through cleaving space, habitus and biography. Joy has a separate room in her home for her sex industry work:

> 'I have a very large [describes residence] and I have little room next door to my study, so one room is for [square] work and the other room is the [sex work] room. The [sex work] room is actually a small bedroom and I've got it split up into two parts and it's much easier when you have a permanent space because the lighting is set up, [details omitted] for the naughty MILF and the [omitted details] horny housewife ... I literally walk into the space and ... I'm ready!'

Helen has a similar strategy: "I try and keep my day job different from escorting in terms of having a separate bedroom for working from or different premises. And that helps me to kind of block things off." Alice has a room for sex work and has no-go zones where clients cannot enter to separate her work and life: "I don't have clients in my lounge. I used to do that. Sit them down and show them around and give them a cup of tea. I don't any more … I think part of me does that to separate it a little bit." Similarly, Wyatt demarcates client space from his life space in his home:

'People always say "oh it must feel weird to do [sex] work at home" but it's such a defined space. The clients are only in the bedroom and the bathroom, and they're never in any other parts of the flat so it really does feel like the flat is mine. And they just occupy that space. When I blow out the candles, switch off the lights, put the laundry in the basket, close the door, then it feels like that's fine. It doesn't stay with me.'

After Wyatt closes the door of his sex work room he can shut off thoughts related to that job but not his square work: "The square work is much harder to shut off from because the laptop is [in the lounge] … in the relaxing room, so the laptop is always here. The phone's going with emails. It's much harder to switch off the square work." Juno describes her process of leaving her square job and getting ready for in-calls in the evening:

'I get home I have a shower and make sure my bedroom is totally ready … it's usually like I have an hour before hand to just hang out and listen to some cool music and kind of forget the [square] job and get ready to you know escort … I only use that room when I'm doing sex work.'

She also has a room in her house that she only uses for industry work. This seems to be a trend for many contributors and also signals that they can afford residences with separate bedrooms and workspaces. Alice explains how she arranges her space as we conversed on video chat:

'I call this my office space … the desk in the corner of the lounge … the client walks in and they have a bedroom and access to a bathroom and not the lounge … I do know women who don't like doing sex work from home because they don't want clients in their space. It never bothered me.'

I asked Alice to describe her walk down her hallway, when she is both mentally and physically transitioning between roles. She shared the following:

'I can do it easy now … I can spend hours working at home with one job and then do a client and switch right back into it now. And I would say now I work in my stockings and no pants and do [square job] phone calls, [laughter]! So yeah and occasionally my boss would be "oh let's do a skype call" and I'm thinking "no! I have no clothes on, hang on!" So yeah, I mean I have no problem at all now really.'

Working without underwear on and awaiting phone calls is probably not what Guy Standing envisioned when he discussed the *Precariat* and life on standby! Juggling disparate work and living in the present is challenging. Zaine explains:

'Like now I'm on my computer, and then I'm writing [square work] and that's my problem is like I do both jobs … I'm checking my email for [sex work] clients and so I'm not as focused as I should be on my [square] work. And then I will have a client so I will stop doing my reports, prepare the room, the client comes, I usually do a massage in shorts or naked, but while doing the massage with the client I'm probably thinking about the report I'm writing anyway [laughter].'

Zaine has more of a challenge moving from square work to sex work:

'I mostly do massage now, and it basically doesn't require much preparation. Like when I was doing domination for example or escorting … the way you present is somehow much more important, and you kind of have to put yourself in a mood and dress in a certain way … for escorting or domination if the guy wants to be bottom then I would take Viagra™ for example but then with massage now I can be ready in 10 minutes. I'm wearing sportswear, so I wouldn't even have to change, probably just put some more deodorant and get the room ready so light some incense, close the window, close the curtain and put some candles on and prepare the massage table … I try to look presentable, if I haven't shaved for a couple days I would shave.'

Remi's home is set up for both kinds of work and she manages tasks in both almost simultaneously. She usually sees clients outside of her home and this is part of her establishing boundaries between roles and identities. Remi's home is decorated according to the tastes of her non-sex work persona. She explains her boundaries:

'I've only ever once had a client visit the flat and that was when an emergency happened, and our venue fell through … I definitely don't want clients in the space. It's definitely not decorated as a client space. There is a boundary between work and play. Like I don't work in my bedroom. That's just part of what I think of as hygiene. I've spent enough time in my 20s being self-employed in a one-bedroom studio to know that being able to leave my work space and go to bed is very important.'

Contributors managed cultural identities that were forming and becoming (Hall, 1994) as they traversed work roles in duality. They successfully managed work and identity spatially, by having designated spaces and associated rituals for transitioning between roles in sex work, square work and life from home. As we will see in the next chapter, some contributors chose to put greater distances between jobs and work personas.

3

"I was an escort on a bike": Kora

There are several overlapping themes that relate to identity, avoiding stigma, and managing information and audiences. Role transitioning via commuting and managing technologies are all done by contributors as part of maintaining duality. In this chapter, Goffman's works heavily inform role transitioning, the management of concealed stigma and the Dual-life Relational Paradigm.

Goffman (1959) explains that our social activity involves *performance*, which is action in front of an audience that has meaning for both the actor and audience. There are *settings* and changing locations with props that we use in our performances. Our *appearance* is based on outfitting to coincide with gender, age and so on and we all have a *manner*, which is how the actor engages with the role and fulfils expectations. Our *front* is the impression the social actor 'gives off', their performance of social scripts that dictate how they should behave, referencing the fact that we have a choice in how we present ourselves to others. Goffman posits a *front stage*, where behaviours and actions are of the socially accepted variety for a respective audience, and a *backstage*, where the agent can shed the front stage persona. Stigmatised individuals are surrounded by two types of sympathetic others: people who are also 'discreditable' and in their tribe, '*the own*', that is other sex workers, clients and industry associates; and '*the wise*' who are individuals who are aware of the stigma and help conceal it. The latter may experience courtesy stigma due to their association and proximity to stigmatised people (Goffman, 1963). There is also *off-stage*, a place where the actor can engage with audiences where role expectations are relaxed (Goffman, 1959). Goffman suggests that people are the *assemblage* of adjustments and reactions to the social situations or the fields of interaction that they participate in. This is echoed in Hall's (1994) notion of cultural identity. Duality is operationalised through the organisation of relations wherein information management strategies like these are honed.

Goffman suggests that to avoid extortion and other harms, individuals lead secret, double lives or maintain 'double biographies', a reconstructed life history that disassociates past from present. Goffman's explication of 'double double lives' (1963, p 77) best illustrates my concept of duality: 'The individual who lives a double double life, moving in two circles each of which is unaware that the other exists with its own and different biography of him [*sic*]' (Goffman, 1963, p 77). Constructing a double double biography is necessary and is synonymous with the biographical reconstruction and change in the universe of discourses necessary for macro role transition, posited by Snow and Machalek (1983). The need to 'pass' becomes paramount. The mechanisms involved in passing are best described through Goffman's (1967) explication of 'line', the small gestures, glances and verbal statements that manifest as part of our interpretation and evaluation of self and others in our environments; and 'face', the value obtained by adopting the line expected of you by others. An individual maintains their face when the line they have taken is in tune with their self-concepts and endorsed by others (Goffman, 1967). The face, like identity, is constituted within relations and does not belong to the individual. It is part of their performance. This is an interactional and situated description of appearance management relevant to contributors. Goffman argues that there are lines available to an actor, based on how they present to an audience. One can be 'in the wrong face' when information about them surfaces that does not match the line taken; 'out of face', when the individual does not have a line; and 'shamefaced' when a person is negatively affected by the loss of self-image (Goffman, 1967). Individuals can 'save face' through poise, which is the suppression/concealment of shame or embarrassment and impression management. Goffman suggests that there will always be a conflict between candour and seemliness, to avoid disclosing personal facts that are both superfluous and discrediting. He suggests that most people prefer to conceal and 'pass', especially if they have unconventional secrets, such as Goffman's (1963) example of a castrated Norwegian sex offender who conceals his stigma.

The Dual-life Relational Paradigm

The Dual-life Relational Paradigm (see Figure 3.1) is a way of illustrating the on- and offline audiences and relations that contributors are managing, the *deep acting* (Hochschild, 1979) and the complexities of the field. The paradigm has seven fields of interaction that are temporal, geographical and cyber. They contain *habitus* of various forms, relationships and the biographical information that associates have about contributors. Contributors are the architects of these spaces by heavily shaping who is in them; however, they do not have full control of the capital, information and people within these fields. There are four fields that overlap, described in detail later, and three

Figure 3.1: The Dual-life Relational Paradigm

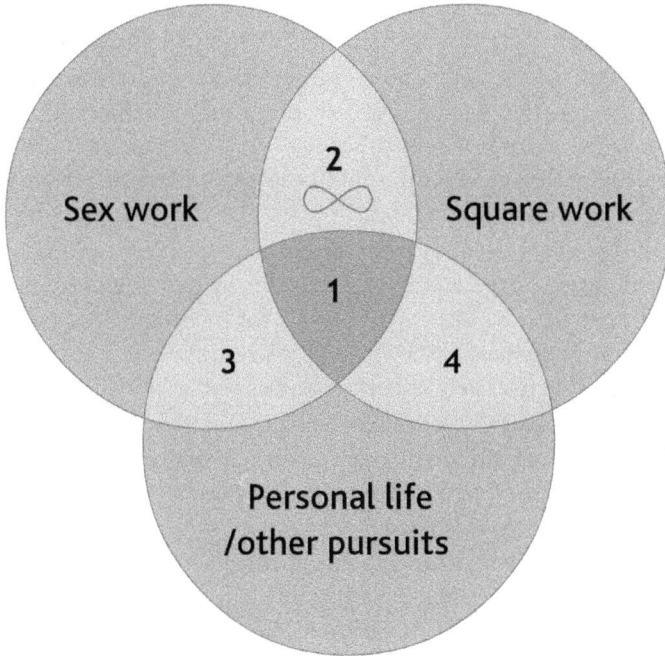

non-overlapping spaces for sex work, square work and personal lives that hold the segregated audiences that are expected.

Relational Field One: Contains the 'Me' (as theorised by Mead (1929)), an inner world; intact plural identities at play *back* and *off-stage*. Contributors may be interacting with the 'own' and the 'wise' here. It is a psychological environment of 'oneness' (Du Bois, 1903; Fanon, 1967); however, this zone holds potentially explosive social arrangements, where relations from sex work, square work and one's personal life may converge in uncomfortable and detrimental ways if there is a breach. The 'own' and the 'wise' are expected to keep secrets, but only if they are aware of this. An anonymous contributor disclosed her sex work to her sister, thus moving her backstage to Field One. She states: "… keeping secrets would mean that we couldn't have a real relationship … I feel a little guilty about telling her because it was a lot to burden her with." Although there is a cost to this disclosure, the contributor now has a loved one who she can be unmasked and unveiled with.

Relational Field Two: The Continuum of SIWSQ Involvement (Figure 1.1) and the Möbius strip (Figure 2.1) are embedded within this field as it is one in which role transition occurs and, for those successful at duality, a balance is struck between worlds. Goffman's 'double double life' (1963), Du Bois' 'double consciousness' (1903), Friedman's *habitus clivé* (2016) and Abrahams and Ingram's *chameleon habitus* (2013) are all at play in this field. There are unsegregated audiences in this field as contributors commute to and from work or secrets may be revealed accidently if square associates interact with sex industry ones. Joy reinforces this point: "... you absolutely have to keep up two different identities and keep these identities separate both online and offline."

Relational Field Three: Personal relationships and those in adult industries can overlap here, causing issues for many who hide sex work from family and friends. Blaze: "I've got a lot of friends ... I think this would be too much of a juicy gossip down in the pub not to pass on." For others, this is a back- or off-stage of sorts if family members know and are supportive of their sex work. Sex industry associates and clients who are friends and lovers will occupy this space. Contributors who participate in sex work activism or sex work scholarship will also have mixed audiences in this zone.

Relational Field Four: Personal and square relations overlap here, which may be benign with respect to duality. This may represent the sets of relationships and forms of information management that most non-sex workers or those who do not manage a concealable stigma are familiar with. Goffman states that people may need to get away from those who can recognise them and who *know them differently*. He shares the case of a call girl who is vigilant about her surroundings: ' "I always look around a room fast when I go to parties," she said ... "I always wondered what I would do if I ran into my father, since he was around quite a bit" ' (Goffman, 1963, p 77). Audiences can be segregated in this relational field, to limit how much personal information is shared and which individuals intermingle, who may know the contributor differently. For example, one may keep secrets related to family life or other proclivities concealed from colleagues in mainstream jobs.

Location, location, location

Off-street sex work occurs in a variety of venues and many people provide in-call services in their own flats or hotels, brothels, parlours and temporary rentals, or outcalls to client's homes, hotels, offices and vacation destinations. Some sex workers do not provide services from home, preferring to commute and do so to keep separation between work and life (O'Neill et al, 2017). Deciding where to do sex work involves finding the most advantageous locations and situations that facilitate increased control over their work since they do not have the same protections and rights as other UK workers. Contributors evaluated the market in terms of pricing for services in various regions and the time and cost of marketing and customer acquisition. Those who had associates in sex work gathered intel about working conditions in various venues, customers, trends and preferences, as well as information about enforcement tactics and safety strategies. Ultimately, contributors desired anonymity.

Blaze considered the following in locating for sex work:

> 'There are certain areas that are well known that have working girls in them ... if you're in an area with lots of young professionals, they are going to be out working most of the time ... it's somewhere residential and suburban, like a house but I would never get a house cause I feel like you're so much more exposed.'

Regional differences were also a concern. Lynn lives and works in a northern location. She avoids locations in the south, particularly London, because she is not willing to invest the time and resources necessary to yield a good income in that location. She explains:

> 'London is a much more cut-throat sex work market. People have to put more effort into their work in order to make money and people also have to work harder because rents are higher. If you put more effort in, you can charge more per hour ... the time thing comes with putting quite a lot of effort into advertising and putting a lot of emotional labour into relationships with your clients.'

Distance, anonymity and risk

Contributors had differing ideas about how much distance they should place between their work locations to keep their worlds apart. Blu (Full Service/Voluntary Sector) prioritised health concerns in deciding where to work: "When I've done outcalls ... cause of my disabilities, the travelling is strenuous but my friend's flat that I use is quite close to me and I would pay them to use it." Helen ensured that there was distance between work sites to prevent seeing clients who could also be neighbours:

> 'My civvy [square] job is only a couple of miles away from where I live. And when I'm escorting, I do out calls in this city as well as going a bit further afield ... I usually do

them outside of the city. So, I try and get sort of like at least 30 miles' distance because I really don't want to have people knocking on my door that you know ... and I end up servicing my next-door neighbour or something!'

Contributors established working flats, conducted market research in areas of choice and orchestrated the timings of sessions with clients who would pre-book.

Kora worked both jobs in the South of England. She provides outcall escort services to clients in hotels and in a colleague's working flat. Both are very near her home and square job: "I went by bicycle a lot to see clients. *I was an escort on a bike* even when I was living in [city]. It was quite funny! ... I often had outcalls close by ... it was at hotels around the corner from where I would work as [private sector]."

Bungay et al (2011) similarly document a sex worker who chose to work at a venue close to home so that she could bike to work. Juno lives unintentionally close to her sex work job: "I'm about 8 miles only [laughter]. So, it's pretty close and I didn't intend it to be that close, but it just ended up that I'm living in this house where I am now. Every time I'm always so nervous [doing sex work]." Juno benefits from the short proximity of jobs and personas but pays a high price for this:

'In terms of being outed, I think it's such a really fine line. I feel worried like people knowing that I'm a [professional] ... working and then sex working in the local area not far from where I live, that's kind of a big risk. Every time I see someone [sex work client] I'm like "Oh God I hope I don't know them" you know.'

Cleo, unlike Kora and Juno ensured distance between roles:

'I do in-calls and outcalls to hotels ... I typically work like two or three days a week, that way my life was separate from sex work. I would just put all of my work stuff into a suitcase and then go to the hotel for a couple of days and then, yeah and then come back ... it was sort of like going into another world.'

Worlds colliding

Contributors shared experiences of what happened when they lost control of information and audiences in Relational Fields One, Two and Three. An anonymous contributor shares a dangerous time in her life:

'When I got kicked out of my home and outed in [date] someone from the [public] found out I was a hooker and then oh my God, I lost all my advertising contracts and clients were starting to pull out. I had no money and when I shut down the [square] business, people were like "oh she's a scam", "She shut down and is running off with everyone's money!" It got out on the internet that I was a sex worker, and so people thought they would make my life difficult.'

Sex workers are often evicted from housing due to morality clauses in some tenancy agreements. Rain talked about a time when sex work and square work overlapped (Relational Field Two):

'I was in a situation recently … it was a meeting with sex workers where you walk into a room and I'm like "actually my life could fall apart." … There was this woman who knew me from my straight identity and I just said to her well I'm feeling ill and I've got to go. I said to like it was a political meeting for sex workers and luckily, she didn't react to it. I ended up with withdrawing from the group completely.'

Rain adds: "This is kind of thing that makes things dangerous. I think many people may not think about it … but their ability to deal with those situations and respond to those situations is affected by a whole set of circumstances and privileges which you may not be aware of." Rain was confronted with a mixed audience in which she could either remain and be outed or extract herself. June explains how her small village gets even smaller: "My clients … I've seen like the check-out guy at Marks and Spencer's, the guy who worked at my local corner shop [laughter]. I mean [omitted] is a really small place. You don't realise how small it is until you become a sex worker here!" Juno describes an incident where sex work and her personal life collided (Relational Field Three):

'I had something stolen from my house and I just left it on the side, and somebody did take it. A client. And I would have loved to like call the police … but I couldn't because if I did that, they would go "why was he in your house?" "What was he doing there?" … it means that if something happens to me or any other girl you know, you can't do anything. You're stuck, so why is that okay? … If something does happen, what can you do? And clients who are looking for trouble, they can come … and they're very likely to get away with it … a lot of sex workers are not out or are in vulnerable situations. They can't you know go to police … It does my head in.'

NUM exists to take reports like these and support victims in finding ways to protect themselves through the criminal justice system or outside of it. Otherwise crimes against sex workers would go unreported and continue with impunity because contributors like Juno cannot involve the police in their lives, even though they are working legally.

Duality on the go!

Containing sex work to a room in a house or a destination establishes a singular reality where contributors can suspend analogical reasoning (Snow and Machalek, 1983), allowing them to fully embrace their roles in time and space. Sage saw new clients and regulars in different locations, however, not only to separate her sex work from her square life, but also to segregate her trusted clients from new ones:

'The regular clients that I have known for some time I see them in my house. I have a second bedroom set up for that but new clients I would see at a different space and sometimes I work from Air BNB. Some of the listings do specifically have "no prostitution" on them but I feel safe using them for new clients.'

In addition to strategically locating, commuting for the purposes of maintaining separate work sites was practised among the majority of contributors. They had to consider *when* they are seen; *as what*, as it relates to their attire/presentation and role; and by *which audiences* and *where*. All of these were core preoccupations. Variations of being in the right or wrong place at the right or wrong time, presenting in the wrong persona could lead to damaging exposures. To mitigate against this Joy commuted long distances:

'I do what they call "tours" and I literally go hundreds and hundreds of miles away from home to [location] and I would do full sex work. I would rent a short-term let for 3–4 days, usually just off a major motorway rather than being in the middle of a huge city.'

Contributors who commuted as part of duality exhibited a mixture of practices of theorised macro and micro role transitioning. Sierra views the mental transition and commuting as an adventure: "I think that the commuting part, whether you just go somewhere in a taxi or you take a train, this is a shift. The geographical distance and that commuting thing, that's where the shift happens for me. You're taken to a different world on an adventure!"

Helen implemented all three rites of passage theorised by Ashforth et al (2000). Her commute is a rite of transition, the shower is a rite of separation and the perfume is a rite of separation that she uses to help her make the mental shifts in consciousness to sex work:

'I drive home from the office and so as soon as I get in, I'm usually wearing just like office gear, so I take all of that off and then … go and get a shower … I have sets of lingerie and underwear that I only ever wear on bookings [sex industry work] … so I'd get into those. I have specific jewellery that I wear … I have earrings which I call my 'whorrings' and my necklace which I call my 'whorlace' and [laughter] I have a specific perfume I wear as well. Even when I'm only doing [non-contact sex work]. I put that same perfume on because it just kind of gets me in that headspace, and all I wear is just my lingerie and my wig.'

June was often rushing between jobs. She explains her typical role transition from her square job to sex work at her working flat:

'If I'm going to the flat, I would just wear my normal clothes. I don't know if there is much of a transition. I'm more of like a super harried last minute, like I could be running in the door and throwing my clothes off and have a client in five minutes. This is like usual for me … I don't know if I have any rituals. I would love to have rituals! I would love to be a lot more kind of "okay and now I'm transitioning here" but it's usually like run in the door and jump in the shower kind of thing … my life is fairly fluid.'

Although June did not spend a lot of time consciously developing rituals for transitioning, her shower between roles is hygiene related and a rite of separation.

Changing on the go was something contributors had experience with. They, often humorously, recounted experiences of changing in tube station toilets as they commuted between jobs. June explains her strategy:

> 'I always have a shower ... I put my shoes in my bag and like I usually change in the taxi. I try and wear something that I can like easily swap in the back of a taxi, so the amount of times I've gotten changed in the back of a taxi [laughter]! But you know I don't really care if the taxi driver knows. I suppose it's a bit bold really, but that's what I do [laughter]!'

For Nova, commuting, changing attire, and mental switching are all overlapping considerations:

> 'I rely on in-calls and I don't go to private residences, so this would only apply when they had a hotel somewhere ... I don't have a driving license, so I always travel by public transit, so buses and trains. It requires a lot of organising to travel, but yeah, I didn't ever feel that I had to change like sort of mentally or prepare, it's more like practical. You have to bring all of your stuff and sometimes I make sure that the outfits for during the day [for square work] are the same as during the night, that I could change just a few accessories. Like from the ballerina shoes you change them for high heels. You put some extra make-up on and you replace the tights for the nice stockings. It's something to think about in the days before, so it takes a time investment to organise all of that.'

Juno describes her rituals of movement:

> 'I get home I have a shower and make sure my bedroom is totally ready ... it's usually like I have an hour before hand to just hang out and listen to some cool music and kind of forget the [square] job and get ready to you know escort ... I only use that room when I'm doing sex work.'

Mary described her commute and role transition from sex work to motherhood:

'I would have a shower after my client and I would clean up the flat, get the candles off and I'll put back on my normal clothes. I've always got my jeans and comfortable shoes ... having a wash, drying my hair and then get into the car. By the time I get home I find that I've stopped thinking about it [sex work] ... There are times when I work too much in a day because I needed a bit of more money so I would do a bit more sex work and see many more clients in a day and by the time I get home I'm exhausted. I find it quite hard to get home and do the washing and take care of the [children] when I've worked too much so I try not to do that now.'

Like many working parents, Mary balances work with family responsibilities and uses her commute to mentally transition and decompress.

From the perspective of relational sociology, duality exists within chains of trans-action that are part of a deeper series of *acting* across environments, where contributors shared the aspirations, negotiated capitals, took risks and competed for rewards in a field. They are actively constructing the intersection between sex work and square work and are bound to this field. Contributors were beholden to the social environments that they co-created. These worlds of relations were protective in that they could manage information to shield them from being discovered, yet they were also at the mercy of these relations and had to engage in self-monitoring, information management and audience segregation to maintain personas and façades in both jobs.

"iPhones are a killer"

Being outed in the digital age presents new challenges for privacy and audience segregation. ICTs play a significant role in our work and socialisation. Trottier (2012) highlights four dilemmas relating to the uptake of social media: how individuals use platforms; how institutions aim to control individuals; the ways that law enforcement access content; and the monetising of our online lives by marketing companies. The first three dilemmas relate directly to contributors' online work and potential risks. Trottier warns that an unintended consequence of sharing our lives on social media or online dwellings is their potential to surveil. He characterises this surveillance of our online lives as unceasing and enduring, consistent with 'panopticism' (Foucault, 1995), where we operate under the unyielding, omnipresent gaze belonging to corporations, governments and intelligence agencies. For many of us, our interactions, work and identities are digitally facilitated. For contributors, technologies both supported and challenged their abilities to control on- and offline personas and conceal stigmatising information. Increasingly, platforms and software from the Facebook™ family of companies, Twitter™, Linkedin™, Apple Inc. ™, Fitbit™ and Google™ are making anonymity online a thing of the past. Beyond social and functional aspects, platforms and digital services have become mechanisms for the mining and harvesting of information ('big data'), in real time, about our preferences, habits and contacts. This information is used to predict human behaviour and inform commercial aims, in addition to improving strategies for surveillance and social control.

Those living dual lives must constantly manage audiences and on- and offline information in all seven fields portrayed in the Dual-life Relational Paradigm. Dangerously, technologies can facilitate a mixing of audiences by pulling associates and information in from sex work, square work and personal lives to the four relational zones where these worlds overlap, with the added dynamic of exposing online personas, work and information. Goffman (1963) states that those who may not know that information they hold about a person is secret may out them. Berg and Leenes argue that many social media platforms, by design, impede our ability to separate our audiences and control our presentations and our 'faces': 'Many social network sites cluster all of an individual's contacts into a single category, called "friends" ... it is impossible for users to hide parts of their network of contacts from other contacts ... impossible to restrict access to information to part of their network' (Berg and Leenes 2010, p 1113).

Audience segregation and the ability to control what is known is essential to managing duality. A browser displaying Mary's 'most visited' websites put her at risk:

> 'I think [technology] has the potential to help but actually if you don't know what you're doing, it has quite a dangerous potential to out you in loads of different ways. For example, like I, on my Mac when I open it up it says like "top listed pages" so like [named Adult Services Website] would come up and escorts in [region of UK] and all these adult sex sites when I opened it up in my square work. And I think "oh my gosh." I was sitting down beside one of the [investors] and that all came up ... and it's quite hard to keep it separate from your square technology.'

Mistrust and tech surveillance

There was a general mistrust among contributors about the information that some adult services websites (ASWs) and digital service providers may hold. These concerns will only increase as the majority of off-street sex workers are online (Cunningham et al, 2018) and scandals such as the Cambridge Analytica Facebook™ situation in early 2018 and data breaches draw public attention. Beer (2017) discusses issues arising after Mark Zuckerberg's appearance in front of the US Senate Committee, in the wake of data security issues among Facebook™ end user Cambridge Analytica (Beer, 2018). Experts in data harvesting technologies warn of the pervasive and hegemonic nature of on- and offline information collection, in addition to how 'big data' utilises the analytics industry as intermediaries to gather real-time data to increase the interpretive and predictive power of the companies they serve (Beer, 2017). Data scraping, combined with the integrative nature of online browsers and platforms (Berg and Leenes, 2010) poses problems for contributors who need to conceal information and hide their sex work.

Trottier's second dilemma suggests that institutions have goals for managing and controlling online users. Privacy while using ASWs, protracted user agreements and data harvesting worries have an impact on contributors who work diligently to conceal information and segregate audiences. Several of these ASWs require confirmation of age, location and other information such as credit cards to set up accounts, resulting in the potential possession and control of personal and sensitive information about people who need to conceal sex work either by these platforms themselves or by third parties.

Sierra articulates her dilemma with technology and duality: "On the one hand the technology allows me to do what I do because without a website I won't be able to have this anonymity ... and on the other hand technology works against me." Sierra thought a lot about separating personas online within a climate of surveillance:

'As for technology, I was thinking that because internet is so dangerous right, they are tracking everything about you. I was thinking about it a lot, how not to give enough clues to any side of the line so they can't find the other [identity] ... I was pretty stupid at the beginning. I had one picture which I had on my Facebook™ like a complete idiot, and I did not realise that people can search images ... then I separated it completely.'

Sierra not only has to be content with potentially being tracked through her browser, location features compromise her ability to travel for sex work without her real-life contacts knowing:

'I forget passwords for things so I just save things on the browser, so I can go there straight away. Then I realise that I can't do that … I did not fucking realise! So then I was like "oh shit I have to just delete all of that history every time I'm on any device" and go there again and type the password and try to remember the password. Online remembers everything … it's like fuck off! … You have to turn off the location thing on Facebook™ because you don't want people to know that you're in London: "What did you do in London?" "Why were you there?" So, there are so many traces left online … you're on CCTV everywhere!'

Although online spaces are sites of daily socialisation where individuals can be seen and known through the accumulation of photos, events and other interactions (Trottier, 2012) this is not always safe for people who are concealing stigma. ICTs comprise technologies that threaten to integrate our digital and real-life identities and this has a detrimental effect on contributors who must establish separation between their divergent work roles and personal lives.

Here in the UK, efforts have been made to increase accountability for personal data among those who collect, manage and benefit from it. On 25 May 2018 the Information Commission's Office oversaw implementation and compliance with the General Data Protection Regulation (GDPR).[1] The GDPR requires businesses, governments and those who control and process personal and sensitive information to be more transparent about data uses and breaches, and promises to increase accountability.[2] Although the Data Protection Act (2018)[3] is aimed to give the public greater control over how information about us is obtained, processed, shared or forgotten by companies and governments, other legislation may work counter to citizen-control of information collected about them. Trottier's third dilemma of state enforcement draws attention to the interests of governments and their agents in monitoring and policing the internet-based activities of citizens. Government monitoring of the internet includes Britain's Investigatory Powers Act 2016,[4] which solidifies state powers to intercept and obtain (tele)communications, and the Counterterrorism and Security Act (2015)[5] section 21 retention of relevant internet data.[6] An evaluation of GDPR and related data protection policies is beyond the scope of this book, but it is necessary to point out that this kind of legislation may not fully protect contributors, since data about their sex working may be 'lawfully' mined and tracked as part of other existing or impending government intelligence initiatives, such as those seen in North America. These include the Protection of Communities and Exploited Persons Act (PCEPA) in Canada, and the US HR s 1865 Fight Online Sex Trafficking Act (FOSTA) and s 1693 Stop Enabling Sex Traffickers Act (SESTA).[7]

In the short weeks following the US Senate approval of FOSTA in February 2018, sex workers in North America reported that the shutdown of ASWs has led to a return to the stroll for some off-street workers (Zimmerman, 2018). Advocacy groups, such as HIPS in Washington and Sex Worker Outreach Project (SWOP), argue that the conflation between sex working and trafficking has led to harmful legislation that will likely cause mass unemployment (Levin, 2018). Groups express concerns around motivations to eliminate sex industry-related online communities in light of the continued deletion of sex worker's data from various cloud-based services and online storage spaces. This US example illustrates the risks associated with online sex work. Trottier (2012) posits that engagement online through creation of identities may contribute to the profiling of users in relation to broader categories such as race, and that this kind of surveillance can 'creep' across other milieus and offer enforcement, intelligence agencies and others access to our information 'for our own good'. An anonymous contributor uses dating sites instead of ASWs to protect herself against intelligence agencies:

'If MI5 is interested in my [sex] working, I would be able to say that it's not a sex work website, it's dating website … I can always say that I'm dating there and who's gonna decide whether the guy paid for my travel and then he gave me some extra money? It's a dating thing or it's a sex work thing?'

Most all contributors in this sample utilise ASWs and social media to contact and screen clients, network with other industry workers, and conduct business in both sex work and square work. The internet was a great resource supporting sex workers towards independence from third parties (Koken, 2012). Mechanisms to monitor sex working populations are put in place under the auspices of saving them from harms such as trafficking and exploitation, but the destruction of vast networks and online communities, many created by and for sex workers to enhance their safety, will increase isolation and reduce the ability to screen and review prospective clients. This erosion will ultimately push sex industries to the margins both online, into the unindexed internet, and offline, displaced to the fringes of our communities and away from mainstream support.

Contributors use several strategies to ensure their privacy and safety online. Nova was concerned about the information requested by websites in the UK to create and maintain accounts:

> 'There are two main websites and one of them is quite nice, and they ask for a lot of things like your phone bill or energy bill, a copy of your ID and I'm not used to that … this [website] is really big and a lot of people advertise on it, and I find it quite surprising that so many people consent to sharing personal data with a website like that. Maybe they feel that they have to, but I don't know.'

Nova also works in another part of the world where people do not need to provide addresses, real names and other identification for ASW accounts. Juno explains that although she must use incognito features to visit an ASW, the site helps her select clients to contact:

> 'When I'm on my laptop using [ASW] I go into a private browser so like if someone was to steal my laptop, they wouldn't know that I was on that site. And when I get an email from a client, you can see how many times they've sent emails to escorts, and how many bookings they've made for example, so before I even bother to reply I just check that they haven't send like 10,000 emails and never made a booking.'

Contributors are reflective of today's working/middle class, technologically savvy, off-street sex worker, discussed in other works (Sanders, 2007; O'Neill, 2010; Bungay et al, 2011; O'Doherty, 2011; Koken, 2012; Ham and Gilmour, 2017; Raguparan, 2017; Pitcher, 2015, 2018). They have online ads and personas as a primary way of gaining clients, receiving ratings and reviews, and gathering information about trends and potential threats in their areas of the sex industry noted in Cunningham et al's 2018 study of internet sex workers. Contributors here tend to be independent of managers and third parties as seen in Cunningham et al (2018), not only because of their computer literacy, but also because they are concealing duality, even from those in sex working communities.

Several contributors used more than one devise to manage duality. Mary explains her device management and the challenges that come with using cloud software:

> 'Often you use the same technology in your square jobs and with phones like with the bloody cloud! I got two phones but the calls they're both going to iCloud even though they are two different accounts. And sometimes when somebody calls me on my personal phone it will come up as their name or like "creepy guy from [city]." I don't know why it does that but that's my personal phone and that's the way that technology makes it less safe when you're living a double life …We're so tracked by technology.'

Daisy (Full Service/Public Sector) also uses the strategy of multiple devices to manage duality but has to explain this to square people:

> 'I have two phones now but I always whip them both out in front of everyone and they're like "why do you have two phones are you a drug dealer?" and I'm like "yeah I'm a drug dealer" and then I go into a whole story about "oh yeah I got this new phone and then I realised that I couldn't cancel this one because I have a contract on this one without realising, but it's cool because this phone works in [home country] and has unlimited data." I, you know, I have to give this whole spiel.'

Daisy uses separate devices to segregate audiences, but a social media platform works against her efforts:

> 'I like having two phones, so the technology really helps because like I've got the work phone which the emails go directly to, and anyone who is a client or associated with a client or another sex worker friend, who's not a real friend all … they only go to that number. And that's really good because Facebook™ is crazy! When you look at Facebook™ sometimes it kind of suggests your friends and if you've got a client's number in your phone they come up as a suggested friend.'

Daisy details her strategy to keep Facebook™ from outing her:

> 'With Facebook™ like I'm trying to minimise my online
> presence as much as possible, so I've made a lot of things
> private and I've changed my name because one of my
> clients was looking for me. The only thing I have is like a
> sex worker support group on Facebook™. That is a private
> group, so you can post, and it can't be seen if you're not
> part of the group, but if you are part of the group then
> they can see my Facebook™. They can see my page but
> I'm not friends with them, so they can only see my profile
> picture which is just a picture of [omitted] and my name
> which isn't my full name. They can't see any of my other
> friends, they can only see things that I like. I've made it so
> that people who are not my friends on Facebook™ can't
> see much at all. But I've got to keep checking that because
> they [Facebook™] keep changing the settings.'

Concealing stigma by segregating relations online also means that,
among other things, contributors cannot blend social capital to
fundraise for projects. Sage explains:

> 'A [Crowdsourcing application] says share it with people
> on Facebook™ to build trust and use that as a profile. I'm
> not able to because some of my Facebook™ people don't
> know about my sex work. I can put my photo on from
> Facebook™ and the [crowdsourcing application] will link
> the two and I can't link the two. So, I can't build trust and
> raise funds. I'm doing something quite remarkable, but
> I can't share it.'

An anonymous contributor chose to avoid a digital service provider
all together:

> 'Never ever use an Apple product on your work phone!
> Apple wants to own your life, so they get their tentacles
> into everything. I would never ever use an iPhone for [sex]
> work. It's just totally far too risky ... now your photos are
> on the iCloud, oh brilliant [sarcasm]! Thanks very much!
> I don't use iPhone at all now. I have an iPad which I loved
> but I don't use it for anything really more than watching
> Netflix™ and reading books. iPhones are a killer.'

Remi also avoids Apple™ products to preserve her duality:

'I'm not an Apple user because it forces a lot of integration that I don't want. Like I didn't get on Telegram™ which is a chat client that synchs to your phone, until I had two phones because I didn't want to sign up for that tool. Then have my clients added to my contact list on Telegram™... like I'm so trying to be smart about that sort of thing. [Sex work name] has her own Twitter™. She has her own Facebook™. She has her own Google™ account. I have two accounts with my domain registrar, so I have a sex work account on my domain registrar and all of the domains that have anything to do with sex work and porn. And then I have another account that I use as my personal domain, for my personal email and my website stuff. I've always kept it really separate.'

Contributors have almost outed themselves using technologies. Alice's main issue in segregating audiences is remembering to tweet from the correct account: "It's just a matter of being doubly sure that if I see something I'm tweeting from the right account because I have so many apps going at once." Lynn does not consider herself to be tech savvy and has issues with only having one phone:

'I'm not like this super sophisticated user of technologies. Like, I have a ridiculous problem of only actually having one phone for work and for life which, is really unusual among sex workers for obvious reasons. That does cause some problems like there's a time when, last summer, when my [pet] went missing. He came back fine but I wanted to put my mobile phone number onto my Twitter™ to be like "if anyone's seen a [pet] call this number" and I felt like I couldn't because if anyone Googled my number it would automatically bring up my sex work ads. Which isn't something I wanted people on my Twitter™ to be able to have access to.'

Blu manages her devices and controls her use of them as part of role transition:

'I have separate phones and at one point I started to try and separate everything a bit more. I tried to like not look at my [sex] work Twitter™ on my normal phone ... I've tried not be accessible [for sex work] all of the time, so if I was going out for the evening with my friends I would not to take my [sex] work phone.'

Similarly, June began the practice of turning her sex work phone off as part of her role transition:

'I remember in the beginning I wouldn't remember to turn my phone off when I got home ... I'm seriously technologically challenged, so you know technology is great, it allows me to do what I do and be independent. I love technology for that, but I'm so challenged. And the worst thing is like, every time I need to figure something out my kids show me on my [sex] work phone. I'm completely lost. I had two separate phones because I'm so disorganised and a bit chaotic.'

Helen not only manages her devices, but all items on her person that could out her:

'You know I'm very careful about not taking any identifying documents or anything out with me like if I go on an outcall. I don't take my civvy [square] phone. I don't take my purse with any of my credit cards in it or anything. So, if a punter was to rob me or if I was to get in an accident you know, I wouldn't be identifiable ... When I webcam I wear a wig. I don't show my face in free mode, and I don't show my face on any of my advertising pictures. That's probably the hardest part for me ... is retaining that anonymity and you know you do kind of think to yourself "what would happen if I went to an outcall and it happened to be a colleague?"'

The risks associated with having access to technologies, and the strategies to manage devices in ways that support anonymity and safety are well known among sex workers and support services around the world. When I worked providing support to sex workers in the Downtown Eastside of Vancouver BC, for example, we helped collect cell phones over the years so that street-based sex workers could at least call 911 (police and ambulance emergency services number in Canada) if they were in danger. Students at Simon Fraser University supported later incarnations of this initiative.[8] Similarly, in 2019, Sex Worker Advocacy and Resistance Movement (SWARM) in the UK initiated their 'Dialtone' Project, which provides first and second phones to sex workers to help them manage their work and lives (Newton, 2020). Device management supports the separation of sex work from personal lives, or in the case of contributors, to separate work roles from each other and from their personal lives.

Although the digital world has moved on since Trottier (2012) and Berg and Leenes (2010) shared concerns about surveillance, commodification and audience segregation on social media platforms, the issues that they draw attention to still resonate with contributors. These include the risks inherent in using some operating systems (OS/IOS) and social media platforms that collect and triangulate personal information including images, contacts, biometrics, purchasing practices, location data and more. Some social media platforms offer features that bridge online identities and life-worlds with offline ones, to the dismay of anyone who wants a healthy separation between work and personal lives, let alone to utilise ICTs to conceal stigma. Trottier's (2012) example of Facebook's™ 'check-in' service, which allows users to geo-locate themselves to their online networks, causes problems for sex workers who tour. Contributors must continuously explore the features of the digital services they use and stay abreast of changes in terms and conditions that may opt them into features that put them at risk of being outed. Keeping worlds apart, and managing relationships, information and power within the Dual-life Relational Paradigm is an active preoccupation. The pressure of it all takes its toll on some who choose not to be online outside of work identities. Joy explains:

'I've no personal social media at all … I've never been particularly interested in it. I've obviously got a [square work] social media account, but in terms of the sex work, it's simply a [ASW] profile. When I go to [region of the UK] to work, I put up an escort profile and that's it … I have one email address for work, one for sex work, and I have a laptop for sex work … I don't have a Facebook™ profile or anything at all like that. I just keep it completely and utterly separate.'

ICTs have undeniably transformed our interactions. We can now have broader experiences of the world at our fingertips. The internet, social media, and existing and emerging technologies present opportunities to expand networks, conduct business, as well as change how we can present ourselves to publics; however, there are heightened risks to sex workers having devices. UK sex workers are not alone in their worries about the harms of using devices, as counterparts in India too have had cell phones confiscated by police. Sex workers in India have had their clients contacted by police to be witnesses in bringing charges against them (Kaushik, 2019). For UK sex workers, engaging with online dwellings such as ASWs, WhatsApp™ groups, and joining safety apps and platforms such as NUM and Client EYE, which help workers screen dangerous people and time wasters respectively from personal devices, is not advised. Both NUM and Client EYE are services that utilise technologies to reduce harm and provide tools for safety for sex workers but pose risks for those living dual lives as well as for those who do not have separate devices for sex work and square work, who need to compartmentalise sex work from square profiles. Contributors shared concerns about the risks that ICTs pose and how they manage devices to reduce emotional labour and distance themselves from work. Contributors diligently managed online profiles and audiences to avoid outing themselves and safeguard themselves against stigma and protect their loved ones from courtesy stigma. As a positive, technology, when well managed, provided greater access to clients and support networks, as well as access to tools, tips and strategies to improving health, safety and working conditions.

Trottier (2012) contends that social media has forced a redefinition of public and private information. People wrestle with the pressure to be visible and the need for privacy; however, they develop public profiles and online networks with institutions and workplaces in both jobs to be marketable. There are several activities that make using technology to manage duality challenging, and these include: the enactment of SESTA/FOSTA in the US and the ripple effect this is having in the UK; the capacity for online monitoring and data harvesting/scraping seen in the activities of Cambridge Analytica; spying practices exposed by whistle-blower Edward Snowden[9] about the US National Security Agency (NSA); and the admission by UK police officers that despite not being properly resourced they were 'considering, or had already commenced some form of scoping exercise into internet-based sex work … and some had already undertaken their own mapping exercises' (Sanders, et al, 2018, p 135). Contributors adapt sophisticated strategies to 'go grey'[10] and avoid being the targets of the enforcement gaze. Sanders et al (2018) document the use of pseudonyms, separate work and personal profiles, hiding identifying body parts, and using virtual private networks (VPNs) among online sex workers in their sample.

Unfortunately, the tactics used by contributors to segregate audiences and devices, avoiding integrating software, may prove ineffective in reducing the panopticism of the state and corporations as there is an appetite for increased monitoring of online dwellings and (in)direct criminalisation of sex workers. Some are resisting by establishing worker-only groups on existing platforms and launching their own social media communities such as SWITTER[11] for example. The outcomes of these activities are yet to be seen; however, the need for user control of audiences and the separation of social identities will continue to grow.

Contributors did all they could to keep their worlds apart. Most commuted to put geographical space between their jobs and some who worked from home created spatial and psychological boundaries and area restrictions to manage sex, work and personal lives. Some even used candles and perfumes to change mental states in preparation for roles. Implementing some macro and micro role transition techniques in their presentations of self, complete with separate attire ('whorrings' and 'whorelaces') to ensure that front stage, line and face were adequately performed. Goffman's (1967) dramaturgical model of social life was alive among contributors. Transitioning between sex work, square work and personal lives while segregating audiences and managing information and ICTs is a profound movement of *being*. Goffman states that social life is about 'moments and their men [*sic*]' (1967, p 2). Duality is proving to be about managing liminal space, the gap between moments, identities and work.

In the next chapter, contributors share insights about Brexit and work. The UK whorearchy materialises and reshapes the sex industry.

4

"Maybe it will be good for British girls because less Europeans coming into the industry": Darcy

The EU referendum

On 23 June 2016 a referendum was held allowing the UK public to advise on leaving the EU, known as the Brexit vote. It may seem odd that Brexit features in a study of the most hidden populations of off-street sex workers. Brexit was a prominent theme in the research due to the timing of the data collection phase in the UK between 2016 and late 2017. Sex workers are not considered when assessing the potential risks and benefits of geo-political decisions such as leaving the EU yet what occurs in the political economy affects all workers whether their contributions are recognised as part of formal marketplaces or not. Contributors discussed how Brexit would affect their work. They talked about race, or more accurately, culture and citizenship as phenomena that influenced their earning potential and the way they marketed themselves. Some contributors worked in the EU and shared a sense of uncertainty about how that would continue. Juno, for example, worried about her tax status:

'I work in [the EU] … And when Brexit happens I'm not really sure what will happen, like I get a sex worker's permit from the government, just for tax, and to do that you have to have an EU passport. I mean in a few years if I'm not going to have an EU passport then that would certainly affect me … I pay my taxes and I don't think they give a crap as I'm paying. They see "oh you've got a British passport" and here is your registration tax number, and if you make more than so many euros you start paying tax. But I mean I was really nervous that that was going to trickle through and become a problem for me in the UK, but I've been doing it for years and nothing ever happened.'

Brexit has been characterised as a protest vote in response to years of Conservative government austerity measures that most profoundly affected working class families residing in the North of England (Seidler, 2018). European and non-European immigrants were portrayed by some in the right-wing media as a threat to Britishness. It was reported that some working class people felt that due to globalisation, London, as the seat of Britain's political elite, was no longer part of, or working in the interests of, 'their country'. Seidler explains:

> London itself was being transformed into a global, multicultural and multi-faith city ... There was an awareness that London existed as another country – experienced by many living in traditional areas of the North of England as if it had become a foreign country that they could no longer relate too [sic]. (Seidler, 2018, p 23)

Although the Brexit vote can be understood as a class war between working class protectionist Northerners and the globalised South, the focus here is not to debate this, instead it is to acknowledge that Balkanism, racism and xenophobia, better known as 'project fear' (Seidler, 2018), made the UK whorearchy visible as a central organising feature of the off-street sex industry among this sample of working class sex workers. Contributors voiced concerns about Brexit's impacts on the UK economy in the context of the xenophobic anti-European/anti-immigrant discourses that permeated the public domain at that time.

The pound had dropped to a 31-year low[1] in 2016 as a result of fears associated with the vote to leave the EU; there was a spike in hate crimes,[2] and an increase in reporting these harms in England and across the UK. Contributors were responding to potential instability and interruptions to both of their revenue streams.

Brexit and (sex) work

Contributors had a general worry about their square jobs. Franco worried about how leaving the EU would affect both his jobs:

> 'When it [the referendum] first happened I started crapping myself, I mean really fucking crapping myself ... what hit me wasn't the job I do but it was just that I am a business man and a small trader and thinking decisions like these affect small businesses first. Work was pretty quiet for a few

days after the vote … but I misinterpreted it and said, "oh my God, now people won't spend money on sex", cause sex is a luxury. But I forget this on a regular basis, people will always pay for sex!'

Helen believed that the vote to leave the EU had a great effect on her square job:

'It's had an effect on my civvy job because our share prices crashed the day after. I don't actually have any shares because [omitted] but there were some long faces in the office the next day … Some of the [co-workers] who have been there for 15–20 years you know … like 40% was wiped off of their investments … it has recovered now but it's still not where it was.'

Contributors considered impacts and developed contingency plans, but not everyone was worried. Joy compared Brexit to the Scottish independence referendum, which took place on 18 September 2014, in which a vote for independence from the rest of the UK was sought and lost by a margin of just over 10 per cent.[3]

'I don't think it [Brexit] will affect my mainstream job at all. And I think that eventually everything will settle down. And in the political turmoil and political change, like we had that here in Scotland with the referendum and it was very very close, a very close vote and people were talking about change but everything has a pretty steady pace, and the world will still turn around.'

Migrant workers in the study had a range of concerns. Nova had concerns about funding for her square job:

'I was most worried about my [EU funding for square work] but my [omitted] said it's okay don't worry and I have it for 4 years and I signed for it anyway. It might change for future generations but anyone who already started can continue so there's no problems in terms of that but I'm not sure if after that I might not have the right to work in the UK anymore. But I don't know what the consequences are for [square job] but maybe sex work would be legal, so maybe I would be a legal migrant sex worker!'

Kora states: "I will die if I can't stay in the UK ... it's going to diminish my income!" Similarly, Daisy was concerned about how Brexit would affect her sponsorship:

'I got an email from my union telling me not to worry about Brexit, that it should be okay but there might be changes in terms of like ... cause I'm on a sponsorship. Brexit will only affect me if it changes the rules surrounding sponsorship from people from non-EU countries, so I don't really know. Worse comes to worse I could marry my boyfriend who is British. I would honestly do that just to stay here because for me going back to [home country] is out of the question like I can't live back there anymore.'

And her sex work:

'With [sex work] no I don't like maybe at the start it would be bad because I think the pound dropped. So I think there was less work, but for me because I wasn't like consistently doing sex work and I didn't see the difference, but I imagine that for those full-time workers who were like starting to realise what the patterns in the market are like. It dies down at the end of the month and then goes up again on pay day, so they may have noticed it more ... But I have been able to at least get work [sex work] once a week.'

Juno explains how the loss of EU citizenship will affect her sex work there:

'I work in [European city] sometimes in the red-light district and occasionally, usually a couple of times a year ... And when Brexit happens I'm not really able to do that because to work in [European city] you have to get a permit, like a sex worker's permit from the government just for tax, and to do that you have to have an EU passport. I mean in a few years I'm not going to have an EU passport you know.'

Some contributors were emotional about the decision to leave the EU as it affected rights, identity and belonging. Cat (BDSM, Porn/ Private) stated:

'Me and most of my friends have been massively emotionally shaken up because of it … London pride was the day after the result and you could feel the heaviness in the air because people knew that things were going to change, and it was hung like a really bad omen in a way. And at work [square] I've had lots of meetings with lawyers and things about Brexit and I don't know I think in terms of legislation it might affect the way things are. In day to day terms I haven't really noticed a difference on the sex work side but yeah, I think it's got a big impact.'

Cat adds that working in the industry in the UK may be more challenging because the EU influence brings progressive perspectives:

'Europe is more progressive when it comes to sex work than the UK is. I know that there's that parliamentary committee that kind of put through … the home affairs, I mean when you consider the number of countries in Europe where it's decriminalised and very legal, I think we might suffer from not having that influence.'

Remi similarly commented on the progressive politics of the EU as a great loss in terms of culture and her identity:

'The UK has always been a pretty authoritarian, conservative country and xenophobic, and mourning for its colonial past and wanting to carry on bullying the world and not giving anything back. Being part of Europe moderated that and the diversity and cultural enrichment improved our communities, and I just think it's tragic that we're going backwards. I've always considered myself a European citizen and I feel like I've been stripped of my citizenship without my consent.'

Remi adds that having access to EU courts as a sex worker had provided better protections for her as a worker:

'In terms of the laws surrounding my work, every time there's a bad law or a breach of the law in the UK from law enforcement or government, the EU has got my back! Like I've been able to appeal to the European court of human rights and say that "this is a breach of the European convention".'

Mary states that Brexit has already had a negative effect on clients' spending habits: "It's definitely impacted on people's financial security I guess, and people aren't willing to spend as much money but hopefully it won't last for long." When working in her square job, Mary was recently in Europe and she pondered the loss of her European identity:

> 'It might affect in terms of the travelling I do in my square job it might make it a bit more difficult for example when Brexit happened and the vote happened and I was in [Europe] at the time and it was ... I felt horrible to then be in Europe and to think that we then couldn't call ourselves European ... You don't feel that sense of being at home in all of Europe.'

European identity was also important to June, who comments:

> 'The biggest thing that I find upsetting is that I love like the "international-ness" of my group of [co-workers in square job] ... so I find that a bit troubling to think that our work together might not continue. I'm so like really kind of torn about Brexit. I do think like I like the idea of local autonomy and ... I don't like the idea of autonomy being given away to somebody that you don't even know who they are ... And I love the free movement, so I'm really conflicted about it.'

Contributors' reflections about how Brexit would affect their work and identities is also linked to a UK whorearchy of white sex workers with respect to citizenship.

Hierarchies

Hierarchies and dichotomies based on biological and socially constructed differences, from which whorearchies emerge, put characteristics in relation to one another. Doing so usually establishes, and sometimes reveals, power dynamics that have been dangerously skewed to favour those who created the hierarchy in the first place. Samuel George Morton's racial ranking of cranial capacity is a good example. Morton, the founder of scientific racism, divided humans into five independent racial categories. Predictably, white people occupied the top of the hierarchy as the most intelligent humans and black people the bottom (Gould, 1978). Other hierarchies and ranking systems include the Madonna-Whore dichotomy (Freud, 2001), which distinguishes virtuous women from promiscuous ones. In 1910 Sigmund Freud wrote: 'The woman's value is measured by her sexual integrity and is reduced by any approach to the characteristic of being like a prostitute'[4] (Freud, 2001, p 167).

Joy commented that there is a hierarchy at play in sex work, where women are ranked according to levels of chastity: "I think men have this almost sort of hierarchy of what they perceive as being the chaste virtuous woman with the mother, being the pinnacle of the chaste woman, a virgin, down to their wives and daughters and then there's the bottom level of the whore."

The whorearchy as a concept is not originally my own and generally denotes a valuation of sex workers against characteristics that are preferred among clients in their respective marketplaces. A sex industry hierarchy or whorearchy has not been documented in academic literature outside of sex hierarchies. For example, Rubin (1992) envisages a 'sex hierarchy' reminiscent of Freud's work, where good, normal sexuality among married, heterosexual people, done for free in private, is juxtaposed with bad and abnormal activity that is done among the unmarried, possibly alone or outdoors. Good performances of western femininity were not enough to deflect a bad girl taint among UK dancers against a chastity-based gender hierarchy (Mavin and Grandy, 2013). There are several research studies that capture demographics of samples and themes related to gender, race, pricing and client preferences but no empirical study has yet been conducted to explore a full UK whorearchy.

Whorearchies

Thankfully, sex workers have been discussing whorearchies for some time. Belle Knox (2014) wrote about the whorearchy in *Vice* (Lieb, 2016), and it was discussed by a well-known UK sex worker Charlotte Rose on her radio show in February 2017. Noted commentator Maggie McNeill (2012) discussed it as well. A whorearchy was illustrated by Monique Duggan in 2016, depicting types of sex work in a pyramid. The stratification was based on the degree of contact sex workers had with clients and police. Duggan placed Cam girls at the top, followed by strippers, sugar babies, dominatrices, indoor sex workers and, at the bottom stratum, street workers. Tilly Lawless, a

US-based sex worker, places sugar babies or sugaring (Nayar, 2016) at the top of her hierarchy because their sexual exchange is most socially acceptable and like traditional dating or marriage. Lawless highlighted the high value placed on workers who were white, middle class, cis-gendered women, versus women of colour and migrant workers, who tended to occupy the bottom rungs. She comments:

> The whorearchy comes from both within and outside of the industry; non sex workers will view certain workers as dirtier/more disposable/less worthy of respect than others, and sex workers themselves will often throw other workers under the bus, in order to distance themselves from them and make themselves seem more respectable. It's driven by assumptions and prejudice. While you will find people of all different races, backgrounds, genders etc in all different kinds of jobs within the sex industry, racist and classist assumptions feed into the whorearchy. For instance, a non-English speaking, immigrant WOC [workers of color] will be seen as 'less valuable' than me (a white middle class woman) and further down in the chain of things. Often, more marginalised people will be forced to work in lower rungs, for example trans WOC often won't be hired in brothels and so have to do street-based sex work. (Sciortino, 2016)

There is a level of in-group oppression that occurs because one group of workers will stigmatise other workers due to the level of intimate contact they have with clients.

There are historical references to whorearchies. For example, Hodges (1997) reviewed works by Timothy Gilfoyle (1992), Marilyn Hill (1993) and Judith Walkowitz (1992), who all contribute historical information to elucidate 'whorearchies' which stratified 19th-century brothels based on their revenue and geography, as well as race, gender and sexuality of their workers. Both Gilfoyle (1992) and Hill (1993) document that in 19th-century New York for example, sex workers ranged from those who worked in theatres and pubs on the lower end of the spectrum, to small parlours and private homes, with lifestyles and earnings for brothel workers exceeding those of domestic and factory workers of the period (Hodges, 1997). Gilfoyle marks a whorearchy as coinciding with geographical location, race and a dynamic real estate market. Brothels ranged from those located in poor areas, such as interracial taverns on the docks or in 'black and tan' areas of the city were at the bottom of the whorearchy, compared with small establishments near expensive hotels. The entrepreneurialism of wealthy New York families however, appeared borderless, as Gilfoyle documents that some who owned whorehouses in the Sixth Ward slums were at the top of the whorearchy reaping profits (Hodges, 1997). American researchers Brents, Jackson and Hausbeck (2010) cite the work of archaeologist Alexy Simmons, who describes the hierarchy of sex workers in 19th-century Virginia City, where white women who worked from small homes with their own high-end furnishings were at the top; next were two-storey brothels, also occupied by white women; and at the bottom rung were 'cribs', which were where First Nations, Chinese and African American women could be found (Brents et al, 2010).

Colourism

Whorearchies manifest differently across contexts because they are mediated by cultural values, capitals, and subjective and internalised structures influencing preferences, tastes and dispositions. For example, White (1990) describes the emergence of sex work in Nairobi in the 20th century from African perspectives that were resistances to colonialism. The sex industry was criminalised to maintain white male financial control over black women's work and bodies (White, 1990). The whorearchy in this context distinguished classes of sex workers from urban to rural, from street based (*wazi-wazi*) and off-street (*watembezi*), to those off-street workers offering longer-term sexual and domestic relationships that mirrored marriage (*malaya*) (White, 1990).

More recently, research on race and sex work unavoidably captures the whorearchy at work in the lives of sex workers of colour. O'Doherty (2015) describes a whorearchy (though not in those terms) based on racial inequities within the off-street sex industry as a reflection of Canadian society more generally. O'Doherty's research participants described a blonde, white, thin archetype of a sex worker, and those who deviated from these parameters may suffer economically, although there are benefits to standing out from the crowd.

Reece (2015) examined blackness in the adult film industry and notes that black women are not valued as highly as white women. Similarly, Raguparan's (2017) contributors highlight that clients in the better-paid end of the Canadian sex industry tended to be white, and as a result, sex work agents, parlour owners, club managers set quotas to limit the number of women of colour they hire and are strategic about when these women are on shift. Van der Meulen et al (2013) echo this sentiment. Along these lines, Bungay et al (2011) document preferences among those who buy sex for workers with attributes such as English language proficiency. And of the 841 Canadian male sex industry clients who responded to Atchison's (2010) survey section on buyer preferences, 70 per cent had not visited women of colour most recently.

Moreover, a 'whorearchy' structure as it relates to sex tourism has been documented among white male tourists buying sex in tropical settings. Piscitelli (2007) investigated the habits of white men visiting Brazil, who preferred hiring lighter-skinned women because they ascribed to them a higher social status and increased femininity. Valuing women of colour based on the lightness of their skin is well documented in critical race studies and is an instrument of colonial oppression. This process, known as 'colourism' is connected to racism because making aesthetic distinctions and stratifying skin tones would not exist without it (Hunter, 2002). Colourism, as examined by American scholars, is a race-based discrimination that values light-skinned black people above dark-skinned because some white European slave owners preferred and violently produced mixed-race slaves.

Banks (2000) explains that racial discrimination in the US is done when one 'racialised' group discriminates against another and further that nationality, culture and colour are proxies for race. Today, light-skinned (black) people who can pass for white enjoy much better employment opportunities, economic privileges, and treatment (Banks, 2000). In western countries such as the US, colourism is institutionalised such that dark-skinned black people are treated worse than light-skinned people in the criminal justice system (Banks, 2000) and in the beauty industry worldwide, for example, as an exercise in symbolic power (Phoenix, 2014). Colourism has manifested itself in the UK, Europe, Asia, the US and other societies.

The UK whorearchy encapsulates colourism or a hierarchy of whiteness that emerged during the EU referendum, where UK citizens and western Europeans constructed eastern Europeans as being economic and cultural threats to the country's viability and to 'Britishness' – an elevated whiteness. Constructing white people out of whiteness was not a phenomenon unique to Brexit as it has roots in Balkanism. Todorova (1997) documents the 'othering' of south-eastern Europeans of the Balkan states, including Bosnia and Herzegovina, Romania, Albania, Greece and other countries, due to their appearance, 'coloring' and culture. Inhabitants of these lands were referred to as Slavs, dark Europeans and even barbarians by western Europeans from the UK, France and Germany for example (Todorova, 1997). This colourism contributed to how western Europeans interpreted the Bosnian Crisis (1908–09) and the Balkan Wars (1912 and 1913) in relation to WWI and impacts on 'civilized' Europe. Disputes over independence, land and resources in Slavic countries were labelled tribalism because, as Todorova (1997) explains, this term was meant to associate Balkans with Africans and Asians, who were populations also deemed to be uncivilised and atavistic by western Europeans due to appearance and culture.

Dark Europeans and the UK whorearchy

Contributors were very aware of the positioning of eastern/dark Europeans in the UK sex industry. When discussing the whorearchy with Joy she remarked: "[Laughter] 'the hierarchy of the whore' and eastern European women who are sex workers would be at the bottom of the rung." She also noted that there may be pricing increases with fewer Europeans in the UK market: "In sex work, Brexit may have some impact down the line and that could be 12, 14, 18 months down the line with less and less people from Romania from eastern European countries of foreign nationals coming in who are at the lower price levels."

Darcy (Full Service/Voluntary Sector) similarly believes that the sex industry is resilient and would benefit from fewer Europeans: "Nothing ever affects sex work! It's always booming. Selfishly *maybe it will be good for British girls because less Europeans coming into the industry*." Juno agreed that eastern European sex workers may drive down prices for UK workers but that this would have little effect on her income because her clients avoided booking Europeans because they did not want to hire potential trafficking victims: "A lot of clients are very scared and they're very like 'I chose you because you're not Hungarian and you're not Romanian, so I know that you're not trafficked'... I've lost count of the number of guys that have said that to me."

Alice believes that Brexit will have little effect on her sex industry work and on her as an English person because she does not work in the same markets as eastern European sex workers. She states:

'If I was Polish, I would be more concerned ... I also think actually there's quite a large base of eastern EU escorts in my area and they tend to charge a lot less and they tend to work in not particularly nice places where there are several of them. So, the market is different. The guys who see me tend not to be the same guys who would go to a brothel.'

Both Juno and Alice believe that the preference for white English sex workers is not racist but instead about avoiding trafficking victims and being able to communicate. Sterling and van der Meulen (2018) also document this practice of avoiding sex workers deemed most likely to be trafficked among male buyers in Canada who do not hire Asian women. Juno explains the UK context:

'The only reason they chose me as a British girl is simply the trafficking and not because I'm British or they're racist. I get a lot of guys who, they come to me for not just for a quick shag but they want to talk and have that whole like girlfriend experience thing and my first language is English … I'm the same culture as them and maybe they're able to have the conversations they want to have.'

Alice adds:

'… And there is this thing as being British, there are guys that, despite the fact that many other people can speak English very fluently, they have this thing like you know, they want women who can speak English properly … and I'm one of the people who voted for Brexit.'

June acknowledged her race and education as privileging her above eastern Europeans in the UK market and echoes the desires of clients to avoid trafficking victims:

'I know that like being female is not generally seen as privileged, but I know definitely being white is. It affords me a greater deal of fluidity than some … I know that from my education and the country that I come from … people are surprised that I'm a sex worker … I'm not saying that's my point of view but like other people's perception of it … I can pass myself off as well educated, well-travelled kind of like interesting person who isn't here for economic reasons … I know for a fact that people are prejudiced against Eastern Europeans for example. And I know some of that has to do with fear of trafficking, it's not necessarily a race thing but being from [outside of the UK] confers a certain amount of exoticness but "safe" exoticness.'

June lives the reality of her whiteness being valued above that of other white people. Although Sage benefited from the valuing of her non-English whiteness, she experienced xenophobia directly from potential clients who not only commented on her citizenship, but also used their white Englishness as currency:

'The British Empire was busy stripping people of their independence, citizenship, and nationhood so Brexit is bloody karma. Clients say I'm "the right kind of foreigner"… what they're saying is that I'm white and they're comfortable with that. Even clients say they are "white English men" because saying that they were British that could mean anything, so "white" is supposed to be representative of their cleanness and respectfulness and if you reject them they're like "oh I'm white" and I'm like I'm not wrapped up in the colour of your skin.'

Of all contributors, Sage is most vocal about the UK whorearchy, whiteness and value. She did not buy into the altruistic anti-trafficking narrative from some clients who stated that they questioned her ethnicity to avoid exploited eastern European women:

'I am White from [omitted] and I do feel that that's important to say because I'm definitely not British and I think there is a whorearchy up here and being white British is at the top at the pinnacle of that and everything else just flows from it … White British girls who insist that there isn't are in fucking denial. [Clients] are so concerned that I wouldn't be Eastern European, and I think in sex work your value is based on race and the color of your skin and people deny that they're fucking racist and xenophobes.'

Sage highlights that the racism existing in the UK is evident in the coded ways in which whiteness and Englishness are communicated in sex work advertising:

'There are directories that are explicit "British girls" … what they're really saying is that the British are clean, and they have class and are educated and that they speak English. I had one guy e-mail me when saying he was looking at my profile and then he called me saying "you speak very good English for a foreigner."'

As a white woman from outside of the UK, finding a community was difficult among sex workers who denied white privilege or who promoted a false unity among all sex workers:

'[White British workers'] insistence that we are all equal, and we are all part of some sisterhood but to imply that we are all equal does an injustice and dismisses all of the xenophobia and denies the advantages of being white. So, I hate when some people say that we're all sisters when it's a business and a competition.'

Sage not only experienced marginalisation through the UK whorearchy of white workers, she experienced the oppression of the stratification itself being denied.

Freedom of movement

Freedom of movement between the UK and EU was a big issue during the referendum and among sex workers. Magdalena Group posted a blog highlighting that in addition to potentially losing the right to travel to and work in the EU, UK nationals will lose access to rights protections granted under progressive EU legislation.[5] Franco felt that EU migrants were already part of the UK sex industry and restricting freedom of movement may not alter the market substantively:

'We invade a country and we get people from Iraq. We invade and we get people from Syria. It's cause and effect. There are a lot of Europeans working in sex work ... but realistically I don't think [ending freedom of movement] is going to make a difference partly because they are already here and it's highly unlikely that we're gonna deport them. It's likely that all we do is renegotiate the relationship [with the single market] without being in it and we would probably have border, which I find hilarious!'

Alternatively, Helen talked about the impact of freedom of movement on the number of eastern European sex workers in the UK industry:

'If they do stop freedom of movement and freedom of work, then potentially that will limit the amount of working girls who come in from other EU countries to work here and certainly in certain cities. Like in the northeast, you see a lot of especially eastern European girls working, and they tend to be working in the parlors and it drives the prices down locally because they're prepared to work for less. Which is exactly the same as every other form of labour.'

Several contributors commented on how eliminating freedom of movement for EU citizens would affect the sex industry in a positive way, all the while supporting and embracing diversity and migration. Helen shares her broader analysis: "I still voted remain because ultimately, I think that migration is a good thing. I mean I've worked in some industries that if European workers weren't prepared to do the work, we wouldn't have had nearly enough staff because English workers were not prepared to work for minimum wage."

Mai (2009; 2013) studies migrant workers primarily from Europe, Latin America and Asia and found that their susceptibility to exploitation was directly tied to their immigration status. Mai (2013) argues that migrant sex workers are 'vunerabilised' through humanitarian interventions that are fuelled by anti-trafficking moral panics and misunderstandings about the lived experiences of sex, work and migration. Sex worker groups such as the ECP documented harms to migrant workers, for example deportations, in their 2019 report entitled 'Sex Workers are Getting Screwed by Brexit'. Despite decisions of the Court of Justice of the European Union that establish sex work as self-employment, the ECP documents that 'UK police have been giving out notices telling women that sex work is not a legitimate job, that they are not "economically active", that therefore they are not exercising their treaty rights (the criteria for staying in the UK) and are liable for deportation' (ECP, 2019, p 2). The flip side of these experiences of white migrant sex workers in the UK is the negative reception British sex workers received in the Europe soon after the referendum decision. Juno shares her experience:

'The whole Brexit thing, like the last time I went [to Europe] was 2 weekends ago to work there and oh my gosh right, it was awful being a British girl out there because everyone was just like "oh Brexit, Brexit" and I'm like "it's not me that voted to leave the blooming EU!" ... And one place that I work like the girls are just like "oh wow, like why are you here?"'

Juno added that the sex work venue in Europe that she normally worked at welcomed British workers in the past, but since Brexit, things have changed:

'It was just very judgmental and really distant because usually when I'm there they it's like oh, they want the British girl like that's how it works, because it's like "oh she's not Hungarian or not Romanian" and it worked very well for me, but when I was there the other week it was like oh ... a "British girl" [sarcastic] ... It was really peculiar.'

The UK whorearchy

Hierarchies can legitimise exploitive power structures and perpetuate harms as seen within systems of colonialism, patriarchy and capitalism and these informed the UK whorearchy. As illustrated in Figure 4.1, being white British remained the most valuable identity in the UK whorearchy, although the other books may not be in the correct order. White workers in the UK whorearchy occupy the top rungs or are preferred in every type of work. This reflects the privileging of ones 'own' in terms of buyer preferences, and the cultural and symbolic capital that is available to those who are white and of UK descent, or who can at least pass as the right kind of white. Based on conversations with contributors, it is safe to say that order would be white workers, would include English-speaking people of the working and middle classes, with cultural preferences for English, Scottish, Irish, Welsh at the top; then western Europeans; then white workers from former colonies (US, Canada, and so on); then English-speaking white workers from elsewhere in the world; and finally 'dark' Europeans from eastern Europe.

In this chapter we heard of the concerns about leaving the EU and how the sex industry was stratified during the referendum in 2016 and beyond. The dynamics and discourses present in mainstream markets influence people and structures in informal economies because they exist in relation to each other. The regulation of sex industries influences workers' placement in the whorearchy, as police involvement reduces their status and value in sex industries. Migrant sex workers of colour occupy the bottom rungs of the whorearchy, in part due to the 'attention' that they may get from the public, who see them as

Figure 4.1: The UK whorearchy

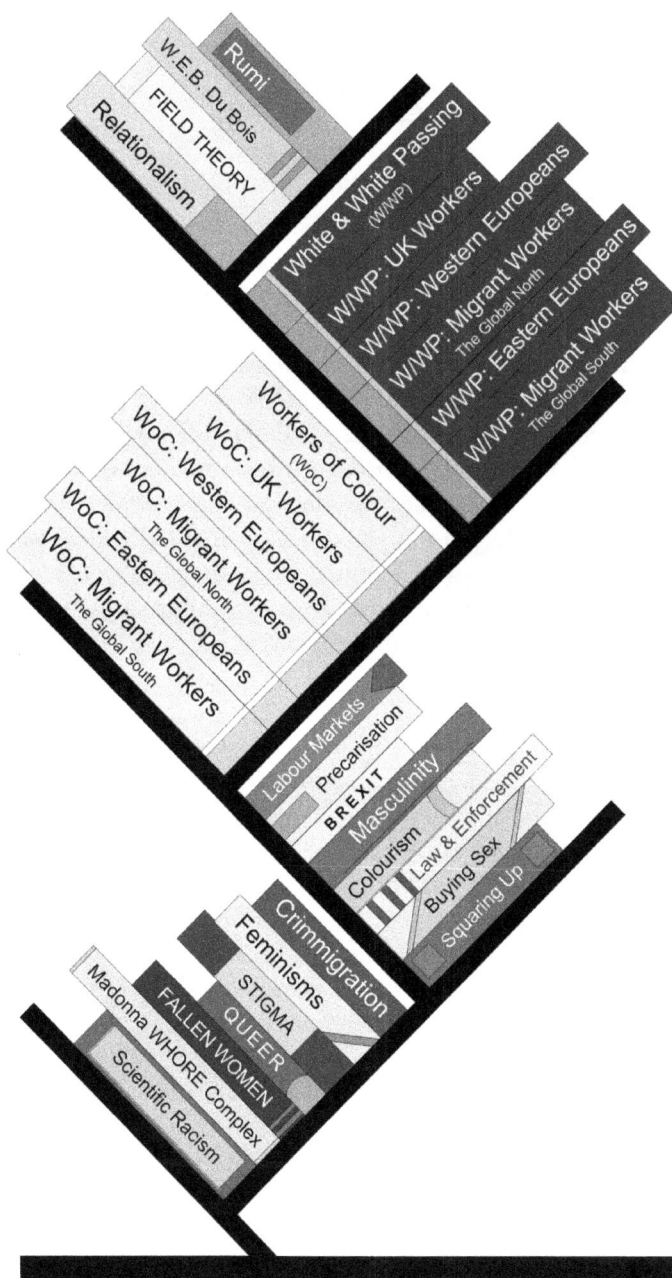

undesirable, and police who limit their abilities to be discreet. Nordic approaches to eliminating sex industries and sex workers through the criminalisation of buying sex have a secondary 'benefit' of targeting workers of colour in predominantly white societies under trafficking agendas that detain and then deport these victims. Criminal lawyer Wendy Lyon reported that migrant sex workers in the Republic of Ireland who experience harm avoid the police. She states that Garda Síochána have a policy of referring these sex workers to immigration (Garda National Immigration Bureau).[6] More research is needed to fully explicate whorearchies that incorporate diverse race, cultural heritages, casteism and colourism; country of origin and citizenship; language skills; class, gender and sexuality; location of services, ways of working and types of roles; police/state involvement in the lives of sex workers; and dual labour markets and working arrangements.

There is an element of fetishisation of exotic bodies as well as a degradation (Razack, 2000) that may affect pricing and 'locatedness' within a UK whorearchy among workers of colour and needs to be examined further as to how differential valuation plays out in the commercial sex industry and is linked to larger dynamics such as the dual labour market. Race, gender, (language) skills, ability, work status and appearance all contribute to employability, and discriminations within labour markets in the UK and the US have been studied excessively since the 1970s (Bosanquet and Doeringer, 1973; Ghilarducci and Lee, 2005; Bentolila et al, 2019). I have no doubt that the underpaying for the labour of certain groups (women, migrants, people of colour, to name a few) in the mainstream will be directly associated with their undervaluation in sex industries because it is the same classes of people with the same old power to impose preferences and standards that do so irrespective of field. The dispositions and *habitus* of buyers, agents, managers, sex industry workers, and the marketers who control media representations of sex industries will bear out.

Hiding what one does for a living is not easy and involves the management of audiences and information as illustrated in the Dual-life Relational Paradigm as we saw in Chapter 3. In the next chapter, we see how contributors do all they can to organise themselves in relation to others in various fields to avoid being outed. This is their greatest fear, and some have failed in this task. Successful duality requires the ability to avoid stigma and deceive others; however, secret keeping has a cost.

5

"I was outed in one of the tabloid newspapers": Anonymous

Media stories that outed sex workers and these contributors are available online in perpetuity and, since their real names were also published, loved ones and aging parents will likely suffer long-term effects. Outing sex workers poses a risk to their livelihoods and future employability. It is ironic that even those who advocate against violence do not come to the aid of sex workers, whom they deem to be victims, when they experience harms such as public shaming. Sex workers are not treated entirely as victims, otherwise stigmatising them would be viewed as distasteful.

A well-known theorist on stigma and identity, Goffman, posits that our social identities have two parts: a *virtual social identity* that is based on assumptions and demands we make of a person without realising it; and an *actual social identity* that comprises attributes that can be proven to be true through interaction (Goffman, 1963). Discrepancies between virtual and actual identities cause people to 'reclassify' individuals based on attributes that are undesirable or acceptable. In this way, 'normal' people assign an 'ideology of difference' and inferiority to stigmatised people and treat them as if they are not quite human. Goffman distinguishes 'discrediting' and 'discreditable' stigma. When a person is known to have an attribute that is undesirable they are discredited, and when the attribute is not known, a person is discreditable but not yet discredited and can decide whether or not to disclose the discrediting information, backstage, to 'the own' and 'the wise'. Discreditable individuals, like contributors here, have a concealable stigma, sex work. They are off-street, educated, working class and middle class, (mostly) white individuals who are situated at the upper end of the stratification with respect to the UK whorearchy, yet they are not protected from whore stigma. Stigma avoidance is a top priority because anyone who has information about their sex working poses a threat to them. The sources of stigma are vast and include landlords, co-workers, friends, ex-lovers, government agents, community services, health practitioners, neighbours and the general public and so on. An anonymous contributor was stigmatised by a despicable group of men:

'I went to buy some drugs and there were these guys and you know they were just thieves, not quite violent criminals but they were doing dodgy shit and I walked in and there were all of these Christmas presents and they were unwrapping them. They broke into the back of a car and stole somebody's presents for their kids, and they were unwrapping them to sell them ... I said "oh what a difficult day I've had" ... and they were horrified. They were like "don't fucking bring that shit in here!"'

Tabloids and media outlets, for example, can weaponise this information to out sex workers, destroying their livelihoods, reputations and families in the process because they believe this to be in the public good.

Passing or concealing stigma is defined as claiming the benefits of an external category of identity while concealing an internal one (Barreto and Ellemers, 2003). Goffman asserts that, to control interactions and information, the discreditable must decide whether to: '... display or not to display; to tell or not to tell; to let on or not to let on; to lie or not to lie; and in each case, to whom, how, when and where' (Goffman, 1963, p 42). People who live dual lives and former sex workers 'pass' for non-sex workers exceptionally well, sometimes too well. Sex workers who pass in a 'square' environment are confronted with mental conflicts as they hear how people truly feel about sex workers and may be hurt by the information. 'Josey' had this very experience: 'I experienced stigma indirectly ... you know that sort of violence of assumed comradery ... I had to just watch people think that I was one of them' (Bowen, 2015, p 441). Armed with information about how their associates truly feel about sex workers, they can improve their strategies to better protect themselves from being outed.

Whore stigma is uniquely gendered. For example, Kempadoo (1999) examined straight, black, male 'beach boys' who sell sex to western (white) women vacationing in the Caribbean. She states that they were not seen as negatively as their female counterparts, instead their work was viewed as maintaining masculinity and reducing the economic power of female clients (Kempadoo, 1999). Women who sell sex are constructed as 'fallen' women in need of rescue by churches, Magdalena projects of yesteryear and exit organisations of today, with the underlying premise of saving women from sin. Adult industry workers are, for the most part, constructed out of respectability and labour itself, although there are some industries that experience less othering such as burlesque, some art and some non-contact work. We saw in constructions of the whorearchy (Sciortino, 2016), for example, that sugar-babying is arguably the least stigmatising because it is most similar to dating, and 'dirtier' workers, such as visible street-based workers and those of colour, are subjected to more stigma and negative attention from police. This chasm between respectability and taint is traversed by contributors as they take up work in both sex work and square work fields. The degree of stigma experienced, and the work required to conceal it, is associated with the type of sex work undertaken, who performs it and who knows about it.

Contributors wrestle with embodied antagonisms between the informal and sometimes demonised sex industries and conventional socially acceptable mainstream work. As tainted workers, these sex workers have coping mechanisms documented in other studies. They have separate work and private identities; work in secret and live double lives; but share information with friends and family who accepted them (Day and Ward, 2014). Strategies used by sex workers to manage stigma include *normalisation*, where workers refer to their jobs as having the social value of other jobs, and *construction of the self as exceptional* (Bruckert, 2012). Ashforth and Kreiner (1999) identified several stigma avoidance strategies used by stigmatised workers, among them the construction of *occupational ideologies* by bringing meaning, value and purpose to tainted work that they do; engaging in *social weighing* to point out hypocrisy and reprimand people for judging their occupations; and making *downward social comparisons* by pointing out the dirtier work of others (Ashforth and Kreiner, 1999). This practice was documented as self-representations and distinctions (Orchard et al, 2012), which may be a way the whorearchies in operation are used by some sex workers to oppress others. Contributors were aware of the ways that they stigmatise others and internalise stigma: "It's probably a self-shaming ... if you've got a straight job as well it gives you like; you feel a lot more credible when you compare yourself to other people who only do sex work."

Day and Ward (2014) define stigma as process of labelling based on stereotypes that cause the loss of status and discrimination. Over time, sex workers in their study had little biographical integration and continuity because they were forced to omit discrediting portions of their biographies. This may signal the longer-term effects of the biographical reconstruction referenced by Snow and Machalek (1983) with respect to conversion and macro role transition. Furthermore, since sex work has not been legitimised as work, stigma continues to contribute to poor mental health (Day and Ward, 2014). Contributors reflected on stigma and its effect on their lives, work and relationships. We return to the issue of identification with sex work. Some did not disclose sex work because of what it means to do so. Kora shares her analysis:

'In order not to say that I'm a sex worker sometimes it's like the covering thing ... I don't see my identity as being any one thing but a very complex mixture ... The thing that is important is that sex work has this stigma and the stigma is very gendered and it's got to do with my identity automatically, so of course the fact that I am now a sex worker and I have been for many years on and off, has probably marked me more and marked my identity more than my [square work] or my university studies or my [private sector] job ... The fact that if you're a sex worker you're automatically denied agency and subjectivity ... my identity is definitely more influenced by my experience of sex work but not so much by the job, more by what it means in society to have done sex work.'

Kora comments on the lasting effects of living in a stigmatising environment:

'Well you know "once a sex worker forever a sex worker" is a big cliché but it is what the stigma is about ... We live in this world which is utterly sexist, racist and stigmatising, and anti-sex worker. So, we've got to internalise [stigma] whether we want it or not ... it's part of my identity of course.'

Joy hides her sex work to protect her identity and square job:

'I don't do sex work full-time because I don't want to lose my identity of who I perceive myself to be. I also need some form of mental intellectual stimulation and I want to stay within the mainstream because sex work is very much a hidden thing, and very much something that I don't want anyone in the world to know that I'm doing.'

In order to protect clients from stigma one contributor calls themselves a masseuse and not a sex worker:

'It's a different type of client who book escorts and massages ... They don't want to be like "oh I'm a client of sex worker." Booking a massage is like a professional service and there might be hand job at the end or a blowjob, so they don't see it as sex work. If I'm in a category of like I'm a prostitute, that puts the client in the well "I'm a client of a sex worker" and it's kind of dirtying it a bit.'

People who work in tainted jobs implement a range of strategies to develop and maintain positive self-concepts and evade the harms of stigma. The denial of agency contributes to the internalisation of stigma, disassociation and distancing from 'dirty' work. Daisy is open about her sexuality but explains that disclosing sex work would be a bridge too far:

'So all of my friends know that I go to sex parties and that I'm polyamorous and they know about all of that lifestyle but I feel like I can't tell them that I'm a prostitute cause that is just way too much for them to process I think. It would change the way that they think about me. It would make them question some things ... when I'm like going on holidays and buying loads of things, and getting whatever I want, I'm conscious of the fact that people may think how is she affording this.'

Not all contributors have been successful in hiding their duality. One was recently outed online and is worried about continued victimisation:

'I think the main thing is the risk of being outed and having people finding out. Like I have gone through that, when people find out they go through your profile ... that is more of a fear for me than the isolation ... I worry sometimes when somebody calls me ... is it somebody that I know that's just calling to see if they can embarrass me? ... there is a bit of anxiety behind every phone call and every person that comes to the door, it's like "oh my God what if I know them" or "what if they know somebody I know."'

Contributors shared experiences of online hate and dehumanisation:

'The most difficult part of the job is the clients ... I've received a lot of text messages that were not nice or that were just plain rude or just stupid rubbish. They have no plans to hire me ... The sex is not difficult, traumatic or anything, the thing the most bothersome are these trolls and timewasters ... That's when you feel like you're the repository for these men's undigested emotions you know. They see you as a legitimate place to put all of their shit ... They don't even think you're a real person ... It doesn't only happen to sex workers; it happens to anybody who's got any kind of public presence or an opinion.'

Helen worries about losing her square job in a conservative workplace:

'I worry about anonymity because although you know escorting isn't illegal, but it's certainly frowned upon by the majority of society. And I think if it was to become known at my [square job] that I escort then there would be consequences ... I could lose my job ... or they would find an excuse you know to get rid of me, because you know it's like an [institution] and you know a "family values" kind of career.'

Likewise, Lynn hides both jobs from family members. She works in third sector health services for sex workers. She explains:

'I kind of conceal both kinds of work from [family] because they inform the other so clearly ... I told my parents about my [square] job and like framed it as like really emphasising the kind of "HIV-ness" of it, because that seemed more legitimate ... I'm sure people in the HIV sector would feel often that they are stigmatised, but compared to sex work, like HIV is so legitimate [laughter]!'

Hughes (1958) posits three taints: *physical taint* related to butchery or janitorial work; *social taint* or courtesy stigma, experienced by people who work with stigmatised populations such as prisoners or AIDS patients; and *moral taint* linked to 'sinful' jobs like bill collectors (Ashforth and Kreiner, 1999). For Lynn, the courtesy stigma associated with HIV was more bearable than sex work stigma.

Contributors varied in the degree to which they worried about being outed. Joy, for example, is very visible in her home community. Her neighbours are not likely to suspect that she leaves periodically to go on tour:

'I don't worry at all because for example, I'm going today actually, tonight for the first time in a while. I'm going down to [city] to an apartment and it's a 4.5-hour drive from my home and if anybody saw me here, I give the perception that I'm fully occupied in a day job and in my [home life]. I come across as being a completely other person, because almost all of my life is accountable … I don't think anybody would actually ever think I'm engaged in sex work.'

She still worried about being outed, unemployment and status loss: "I would be literally unemployable, and in the future, I may decide to take a route of doing some work for government or whatever. Then I would have difficulty obtaining that type of job if somewhere there's a note against my name that I am a sex worker."

This anonymous contributor worried about deportation: "I would have to leave the country because the [square employer] is sponsoring me. I would lose my visa … What am I gonna do like? There's nothing I can do if it comes out." Juno constantly worried about being outed and was hyper-vigilant and stressed:

'It's horrible actually. It's really stressful like, every [client in square job] I get … thinking "gosh who is this person?" "Do I recognise that name?" And then you see things in the media like, people being outed and whatever. It's so horrible … I just hope for the best to be honest. I've been very lucky.'

Duality relies upon the negative stereotypes that people have about sex workers. Beliefs such as the lack of education, drug dependence, poverty, illness, basically variations of three (physical, social and moral) 'taints', make it possible for some to execute duality successfully. Contributors match the characteristics of the mainstream, white working class, allowing them to hide in plain sight. The unlucky ones get outed.

A few contributors in this study were outed by media. An anonymous contributor shares:

'*I was outed in one of the tabloid newspapers*, which was just hideous. I had to resign, it was a nightmare … this forced me into full-time sex work and one of the things was, when I had a problem getting other work is that you only have to Google my real name and the article still pops up on the internet … it made me scared to apply for other jobs because you know companies Google these days and unfortunately my name is unique.'

One anonymous contributor was able to find out who outed her:

'Basically a bloke that I was seeing ... I was seeing him and he was madly in love with me and I kinda dumped him and he started stalking me and then he told me that he had a mate who was a journalist and I thought he was just saying that but then a couple of months after that the [tabloid] showed up on my doorstep and said that they saw my website and yada yada and did I have any comment and I said no.'

The contributor's square job was also contacted:

'It was public sector actually and it was a quite well-known industry and they were not happy when it went into the paper and they thought it reflected very badly on them ... they also rang my [square job] for comment who then, so I was home that day and they rang me and [nervous laughter] I was suspended and then I was asked to resign.'

Another contributor, Alice, was also outed in the tabloids:

'Well pretty much all of my friends know that I do both [duality] actually ... my parents were not impressed when I was outed in [named tabloid paper] ... my parents didn't talk to me for a long time afterwards and they are the only people who l would lie to ... I know some of my father's family saw the article, but it's never been spoken about [laughter]. We're all British, and we never speak of these things!'

The impacts on the family were difficult to cope with according to Alice: "I can cope with losing my job but the effect it had on the relationship with my parents was the worst thing."

Contributors heard stories about others who were outed. An anonymous contributor explained that a friend was outed by an exboyfriend and this has her worried that her ex will do the same:

'One of my friend's ex- boyfriend outed her. He printed a page of her website and posted it to her family and her new boyfriend. That was only last week. But it's awful and I guess it would be the worst thing ever because I would lose my job and I would lose my family ... But my ex-boyfriend like, it hasn't been that long, and I think he only told one of his friends about my job and that's because I encouraged him to because he was having a hard time with it all ... but if it comes out then he's going to lose me forever, I swear!'

One anonymous contributor resorts to wearing disguises:

'When I've been on TV I wear a wig and glasses! There are about half a dozen people who I know who have been outed by the media and police. I don't want my neighbours ... like they could tell my landlord and stuff like that. I want to make that wiggle room between "Oh my God, we don't know what she looks like."'

They also read articles about other sex workers who have been outed. This forces them to reflect on their own practices and the risks they take. Joy shares her insights:

'It's so natural to want to confess, it's so natural to want to sort of you know offload that you're doing this [duality]. To tell your secret to get the weight off of your mind and because by telling someone else you are almost processing what you're doing ... And be your own council but be very careful about who you tell and also I think for a lot of women with children, they really have to protect their children from ... there will be consequences for their children ... [named well-known sex worker activist] who would never had come forward to expose herself, was actually outed by a tabloid newspaper in [region of UK] and so when she was exposed the damage it's done. So now she has to defend herself and part of her defence is to share that she is an intelligent, compassionate woman who cares deeply about people from ... not just sex workers rights but everyone's rights, worker's rights. So that was the catalyst for her to grow and to have courage but the damage that the tabloid press did to her [dependent child] ... and the fall out the emotional fallout from schools and even other parents from school and living in a small community in [region of UK]. So I think people should almost, before they start to embark on whatever type of sex work that they are planning to embark on, to think about it and do the checks almost of checking their parameters and certainly to know what they're doing.'

Liar, liar

Secret keeping in the short term proved useful to achieve goals of stigma avoidance, but over the long term it was damaging to mental health. People who are hiding information may redirect conversations to avoid topics and suppress thoughts about the secrets they are holding, which unfortunately may lead to crippling preoccupations with the secret and obsessive thoughts (Smart and Wegner, 1999). Afifi and Caughlin (2006) highlight that a basic human drive is self-protection, and withholding information is one of the strategies used to keep ourselves safe. They suggest that secret keepers 'ruminate' or repetitively think about their secrets and sharing them does not always yield positive results. For example, a handful of contributors told their families about their sex work. Remi told her parents, and this has not reduced her stress:

'like my life has been so much more stressful since I told them. The net amount of stress hasn't gone down, it's just that they're dealing with it now, not me so it's kind of a selfish thing to do really ... The stigma is there, and I think it's fair enough that they shouldn't have to experience stigma for something that they haven't chosen to do.'

By hiding membership in stigmatised groups people 'pass' but concealing devalues identities and undermines confidence because it requires deceit, lowers psychological well-being, and increases feelings of shame and guilt (Barreto et al, 2006). Furthermore, stigmatised groups face negative stereotypes and lowered expectations of them, and these may become self-fulfilling (Barreto and Ellemers, 2003). Secret keeping reduces intimacy in relationships, so instead of hiding a stigma to increase acceptance, the opposite is experienced (Afifi and Caughlin, 2006; Chaudoir and Quinn, 2010). Contributors have these distant and awkward interactions due to their constant self-monitoring to hide discrediting and personal information, and their need to avoid topics such as what they do for a living or how they spend their time.

In order to keep a secret, one has to be a good liar. Since stigma is responsible for the schism between consciousnesses, jobs and fields of interaction, a good lie is foundational to duality. These divisions of work worlds and personal lives, and the practice of duality for that matter, hinge upon contributors' abilities to construct a version of themselves that is expected in the fields that they trans-act. Contributors rationalise lying as a means to protect themselves and loved ones from the effects of stigma or to avoid the emotional labour of explaining what they do to people whom they do not wish to invest in getting to know. There are different types of lies, ranging from less harmful altruistic fibs; practical jokes; hoaxes; lies of necessity; to fraud; lies to test integrity; plagiarism; strategic fabrications; and exploitive deceit, such as *Plato's noble lie*, which disseminates misinformation during times of war (Meltzer, 2003). Nietzsche states that lying is functional at the societal level because the world is false, and as such, we need lies to survive. Lying is argued to be an evolutionary necessity and is sometimes done to prevent harm. For example, contributors who hide sex work want to ensure that loved ones are not exposed to whore stigma. Lies can have positive outcomes that strengthen social bonds such as those to avoid rudeness or cruelty, and those to support the continuation of the status quo, or to avoid negative outcomes that erode trust. Lies can also promote suspicion, undermine concepts of self, and, at the meso level, challenge the integrity of institutions. Meltzer argues that 'most of us lie as one means of adaptation where appropriate or necessary in certain kinds of situations' (2003, p 66). For Kora, having the ability to lie is an asset: "I'm one of these sex workers who are absolutely able to lie a lot, and to make up stories." Not everyone could lie easily. Tracey (Full Service/Private Sector) chose not to be in a relationship while sex working: "I didn't date. I didn't want to go out with a guy who knew that I was doing sex work and I didn't want to lie." Juno, on the other hand, never told her partners:

> 'I have had partners but then it just gets to the point where it is difficult to do both. I mean escorting is work like I really think it's absolutely fine for me. I find that it's just balancing it all and then you know ... but I have had my partners and I've never told them. Like if I'm seeing a guy in my personal life, and in my head I'm like why aren't you paying for this? Like what am I doing [laughter]? It's totally redundant and all of the emotional work ... I don't even want it. I just had sex an hour ago you know, jog on [laughter]!'

According to Goffman (1959) we do not lie to everyone all the time. Those who choose to share their secrets engage in 'selective disclosure' – revelations that resolve the dialectic tension between sharing information and keeping it secret (Rober et al, 2012). The people that contributors chose to bring 'backstage' into Relational Field One included a range of characters, some unexpected. Wyatt's friends and family know, but not those in academic circles:

'I mean my family know, my close family do, and my square work, like all of my colleagues do, my [PhD] supervisor knows ... like in terms of the [PhD], no one else at the university knows. I don't share with other PhD students, just my supervisor ... and it's just anxieties because word travels fast and if I did want an academic career which I don't think I do, but if I did, then I have to not be out.'

Sierra similarly withholds information about her sex work from academic associates:

'Yeah, my academic world and my family would find out. These are the ones who can't ever find out ... maybe some people would have a suspicion in the academic world ... but maybe it's my paranoia but the other PhD students ... If I hang out with them ... if they put one and one together and they figure out that from my jobs I can't make enough money to survive, it would not be difficult I think.'

A few contributors disclosed duality to square associates: Alice explains:

'It slightly helps that the woman I work for knows about the sex work, which is probably unusual. I'd gotten the work through a mutual friend ... I had a 4-year gap in my CV, so I was quite nervous about having to make up stuff and my friend said to me if anyone is going to be fine about the sex work it's going to be her. So, I rang her up and we had a conversation and she was fine with it ... she knows I've done it full-time and she knows I do it now.'

Alice adds:

'[Her employer] was interested to know more about [her sex work] but I don't think I want to talk about it with her. I think if she had been 40 years younger, she'd be doing it herself [laughter]! She's terribly open minded and ... she wouldn't discuss it. I mean I think her husband knows, but she was really supportive!'

Daisy must avoid telling some friends about her duality because it is too juicy a secret for them to manage to conceal. Blaze similarly states:

'I've got a lot of friends that I'm quite close to and that I know care about me, but I think this would be too much of a juicy gossip down in the pub not to pass on. Not necessarily with my name attached explicitly, but you know how cool it is to know a sex worker! ... especially the fucking middle-class lefties! ... I've got a lot of gay male friends and they love this kind of thing, [laughter]! So, it's not that I think that they would say it maliciously, it's just that the temptation for them would be too large!'

For Blaze, even her most liberal-minded friends cannot be trusted with her secret:

'I have another flat mate who's a guy and I don't want to tell him ... he's like one of these guys that considers himself very liberal and polyamorous and all the rest of it, and I know that he would just lap it up. It would just be like capital for him to say, "oh I live with a sex worker." ... I don't want to be on his lips or on anyone's lips ... It would end up dominating how I'm thought of.'

Blaze did not want sex work to be a 'master status-determining trait' in the ways that race can be, according to Hughes (1945) as that is all anyone would ever care to know about her. Blaze trusts sex workers with her secret: "Well they're hookers as well! We can, like there's an understanding: 'don't fuck with me and I won't fuck with you.' That sounds really harsh actually, but we're all equally vulnerable." Mary has a network of sex workers that she trusts and some family members:

'Other sex workers like know everything ... they know exactly where I work, when I work, what kind of work I do. They know it all, but my [square] friends know that I sex work, but they don't know that I have a working flat for example. Like they think that I just meet clients in hotels or at their homes ... I don't really describe it ... and then there's another tier, like my family knows that I work but we don't talk about it. We don't talk about the details.'

Sage's strategy to managing her secret sex work included a willingness to cut people out of her life:

'You're constantly managing people, and you have to turn your friend groups down into segments: these are the people who know me from this place, these are the people who know me from the other place, so your life is quite segmented. I guess sometimes you just have to be prepared to cut people off and go okay they just found out about my sex work, they have to go!'

For some, audience segregation, on- and offline information management and device management took far too much energy. Instead, they opted to tell virtually no one about their duality. Laith believes that there is discretion around sex working among the middle class, and that this is a feature of being British:

'I'm British, I don't run around and flaunt it [sex working] in the faces of people I know you know ... So, some people know, and some people don't. I'm British, we don't really talk about it. I mean if somebody asks me the questions, they get the answers, but I don't ask about what's it's like for them to be an accountant on a daily basis! ... I'm not running around being American. I'm not on Oprah!'

Blaze also mentioned middle class company as being an environment where she felt least at risk of being outed:

'In the end, no one is going to just suddenly come up to you and say, 'are you a sex worker I think I saw you?'... unless you're showing your face, but even if you are, in polite middle-class company, nobody ... I think it's different, nobody can really challenge you.'

Some contributors do not agree with Laith and Blaze, especially those who have been outed on British tabloids, talk shows and in polite, middle class British society.

Secret keeping is an ongoing process of determining when to tell what to whom, and how to manage discrediting and stigmatising information. Cleo explains this complexity:

'I mean it's hard to juggle being more out cause there's obviously stages of being out, and I'm out in some situations but in others. I just can't be bothered to out myself to people, but I guess it's maybe just to look at like, where the anxiety comes from. Who I'm most anxious about finding out? I mean if somebody can never talk about it, I think maybe you just kind of have to know where those spots are … the people who I know I'm going to see again or spend a lot of time around, I would disclose it, but if it's just like my hair dresser or something I mean I'm just I would say that I don't want to have this conversation.'

Contributors spoke at length about having very few spaces to openly debrief about their sex work. Rain explains:

'The whole Friday night in the pub sort of thing, we have very few equivalents … if you work in a brothel and with other sex workers … there's almost no space for us to talk like that. I think even if we're out to our friends and family, due to the nature of our work … for example I had a situation with a regular client where we're getting to the end of the appointment and I had his dick in my mouth … and his phone rang, and it was his mom! And she leaves this long message about how "I'm thinking about you" and "I love you" and "I hope you're having a good time" [laughter]! And I'm like "what's the etiquette?" Do you carry on? … Do you bob your head? And it's the kind of situation where, like is he getting soft? Is he getting harder? That's not even funny actually! That is one of the funniest things that has happened to me, but you don't want to have a conversation with your best mate or your boyfriend or your mom.'

The pains of deceit

Contributors took great risks to make the money they needed to survive and thrive. They weathered the challenges of having to deceive almost everyone they know and mitigated the risks of being outed to establish income security and social mobility. Deceiving family and friends was most difficult. Contributors talked about their feelings of having to be inauthentic and betray the trust of those they cared about. Juno shares her situation: "My family is like 'she's a [professional] and we're so proud of her' you know and if I came out, I'm not sure how they would take that at all … they're very old fashioned like sex is not spoken about, ever!" Lying to friends and family for long periods made Juno feel trapped in the secret:

> 'My friends, they just know me as a [professional] and I just think like if I came out and say, "oh by the way I've been escorting for 6 years" [laughter], they'd probably be feeling a little bit betrayed that I didn't tell them, which would just make it even more difficult. If I had come out in the beginning I don't think they would have been okay with it, but to tell them after 6 years of them being mates with me, they probably wouldn't think that they know me at all … so I can't really tell anyone.'

There is no backstage for Juno, which makes her duality highly stressful. Darcy describes the stress of lying and her deflection tactics:

> 'It's so stressful and a bit anxious because when people come up to you about this and that and you tell your lies but you're half cringing, but you have to do what you do with kids which is distraction. All of a sudden just change the subject! And go "oh there's blah blah blah" or "did you hear about this?" It's stressful, it's not comfortable. It's like a heart pain … anxiety that's it.'

Contributors experience anxieties about lying to the people they love and also lying to others in their presence. June explains:

> 'It's stressful, I always forget what my boyfriend told his parents about what I do, and I never know what he's told acquaintances and that can be quite stressful … It's the stress of worrying about it when I'm meeting people and I don't like lying in front of somebody who knows you know. I'm out about it with my partner and when somebody asks about it, I feel a bit uncomfortable lying.'

These lies of necessity (Meltzer, 2003) are difficult to manage and the added pressure of lying in front of a loved one is uncomfortable because it erodes relationships by demonstrating how easily and well one can deceive. Having to lie was stressful and not something contributors are proud of having to have done. Alice expresses her concerns:

> 'The stress is unbelievable; it is really horrible … if your main career is important I wouldn't risk it for sex work, but equally I understand that people are in positions where they need the money, which I was at that point. I wouldn't have done it if I didn't need the money.'

As we have seen in this chapter, deception is necessary to avoid stigma, status loss and social death. Contributors manage relations and duality to protect loved ones from courtesy stigma and other harms. They take extraordinary risks to stave off poverty and establish a good standard of living for themselves and their families but none of this was guaranteed. Their jobs and earnings in both sex work and square work were still insecure and unpredictable.

6

"They are both shitty jobs ... because I'm not free": Sierra

In this chapter we take a deeper dive into the challenges, frustrations and fears that contributors have with duality in our current labour market. Sex as a side hustle is frowned upon yet the process of precarisation threatens all work, even for these most highly skilled and educated workers, who spent more time in libraries than they did in pubs. Duality funds 'flexicurity' for them, where there is little safety net; however, they lack protections in both of their jobs because sex work is not fully accepted as work, and they can lose square jobs if their past or active sex work becomes known. Some held jobs in the public trust and examples are used to highlight their challenges here.

Although contributors may betray the trust of loved ones and associates by lying about sex working, they feel deceived by the entire system. In their minds they have done everything expected of them in terms of getting an education and working in mainstream jobs. They stayed out of trouble hoping that they could earn a good living, only to experience a 'dream deferred' (Hughes, 2001). An anonymous contributor shares her thoughts and frustrations:

> 'I don't think that I'm so special and that there's anything special about me ... faced with the reality that you've got no fucking money and there's literally the panic and my parents, they're middle class but they don't have any money for various reasons and so I can't really rely on them. I've done a PhD; I've got lots of educational capital and lots of cultural capital but about 1.5 years of finishing up really ruined me financially. I was always living off the edge of my maximum overdraft and part of that time I was living at home again because there was no way that I could pay rent. I borrowed a little bit off of my parents and then it came to graduation and I literally had like no money.'

This contributor entered the sex industry the day after finishing a PhD. This is the reality for many and makes duality necessary and rational but alienating.

Marx explains that within the capitalist political economy, workers become the worst kind of commodity and are detached in a few key ways: from *products, production, themselves* and finally *other workers*, because their labour and its fruits do not belong to them, but to the capitalists, who undervalue wages and extract maximum profits from their work (Marx, 1844). Marx asserts: 'labour produces not only commodities; it produces itself and the worker as commodity' (Marx, 1844). This idea permeates the conversations I had with people living dual lives. They felt discontent, exploited, underpaid and undervalued in various sex industry jobs as well as in square work. This disillusionment may inspire duality because people are seeking to benefit from their own work in ways the square markets or sex work alone do not offer. Unfortunately, they are still juggling precarious work and, as we saw in Chapter 5, risking a lot. Marx adds that people are alienated from the products that they produce. In this respect, labour itself is a product of labour, and products and services, along with the people who produce them, become 'objects'. The ability to purchase products and services and ascribe meaning to these objects may be a lot of what keeps many of us content. Duality can be a strategy to avoid the trap of 'working to live and living to work' by finding ways to control inputs and *work smart not hard*, yielding the time and money to fund a material existence.

Although many, including prohibitionists and anti-sex work feminists, problematise sex work, some contributors in this sample would not work at all if they had a choice. Lynn discussed her duality in the context of a potential universal income:

> 'I have to work because of capitalism … I'm definitely one of the people that if I had a guaranteed income I wouldn't work. I mean it's kind of hard to say like I would probably still do [charity job], but would that work even make sense if we had a truly universe-based income? … a simple relationship to work where I do sex work when I need the money, and if the government wants to give me a £1000 pounds a month I would just stop … I would just like doss around [laughter]!'

Lynn was mostly joking but also serious. Contributors talked about working in low paying jobs that they hate with the hope of getting an opportunity for a better life.

'The more objects the worker produces the fewer he can possess' (Marx, 1844). By this logic, the more one works the less one has. Since labour is external to the individual and belongs to someone else, in Marx's estimation, it is an activity that is non-affirming. Sierra discussed her experiences on a zero-hours contract alongside sex work:

> '*They are both shitty jobs*. It doesn't matter whether you exploit your body or whether you exploit your smiling face, both are exactly the same *because I'm not free*. They are just types of exploitation you know … like being on a zero-hours contract, they're relying on my being smiley and pleasant and listening to shit from people, which is exactly the same like the other job [in sex work]!'

Marx's concept of self-estrangement and *species-being* relates to the immaterial and spiritual aspects of being free in nature. Alienating humans from nature makes it so that 'life itself appears only as a means of life' (Marx, 1844) as utility … for its own sustenance. Beyond this life activity is conscious life activity that separates human beings from animals, making mankind a *species-being*, consequently estranging us from our *species-life* (all of humankind's universal production) alienates us from ourselves. Duality may contribute to disillusionment as alienation must be more profound when one's work is not recognised or universally accepted as work. Shah (2009) highlighted that sex workers are constructed outside of society. Their contributions are easily erased, just like those of unpaid (mostly women) workers, who run households and take care of families, who nurture the workforce and the student body.

In February 2019 the Trade Union Congress (TUC) documented that 850,000 UK workers were trapped in zero-hours contracts, 715,000 living in England, with the highest percentage being in the North-East (Klair, 2019). Zero-hours contracts are critiqued for their erosion of workers' rights and the exploitation experienced by those forced to work this way. They are a form of legislated poverty and most of these jobs are in accommodation and food industries. Sierra jokes about both jobs being in customer service and the alienation she feels as they both also benefit from her appearance and require her to do 'face-work':

> 'I mean both of them [lists jobs in sex work and square work] are like horrible and I'm someone else in both of them. Neither is worse than the other … hopefully there

will be a day where I can stop both of these ways of working
… it's also what they want in customer service, you have
to have makeup on … the visual is important.'

Considering the high debt-load that Britons carry according to the
Office for National Statistics (2017); the ever-widening wealth gap
(Office for National Statistics, 2018); and the feminisation of poverty
among sex workers noted in decades past (Scambler et al, 1997),
choosing duality is rational and logical for some. Duality for flexicurity
in the sense that McKay et al (2012) meant it involves financial
resources being provided by governments for temporary workers who
are between jobs and funding for training. This serves to maintain the
gigging economy without making people destitute. For contributors,
duality provided the backup resources necessary to pay bills, pay for
training and education, and maintain basic lifestyles when there were
gaps in revenue from either sex work or square work. Alice explains:

> 'I thought that I wanted to give up sex work, that was my
> goal, but then I realised that I didn't … I have an income
> from elsewhere, I can be a lot choosier about who I see.
> The desperation … not desperation, but the need isn't there
> as much as it was previously because I would get a lump
> sum at the end of the month from my other work … there
> isn't quite the urgency to do sex work … I've been around
> 7 years I have a lot of regular clients, so I don't have to see
> new men very often. It's really changed how I work.'

Alice was able to do sex work in the ways that were safest for her
because she could rely on square income when she needed to. Her sex
work is precarious, but it is not survival work because of duality. As
a parent, duality allows Mary the flexicurity she needs yet she desires
to hold one job that earns her liveable wages:

> 'I feel like at the moment it's good to have both [duality]
> but what I would like in the future is to have a straight job
> that afforded me enough to just pay all of my expenses and
> enough time with the kids and the family … Like being a
> mom and doing this is ideal because you can pick your own
> hours, there isn't a set thing. If your kid's sick you don't
> have to go into work, not having a boss, and there's all the
> kinds of flexibility that comes with sex work and [being
> an entrepreneur in square job].'

Escaping poverty is not just having a good job, it is acquiring the assets needed to build wealth. For Helen, and 68 per cent (n=17) of the sample, duality is done to achieve a specific project or goal, with an end in mind. Helen discusses her plans to take part in the government's 'Affordable Home Ownership Scheme' with an individual savings account (GOV.UK, 2018).

'I want to escort and do civvy [square] work for at least the next year, but I've got a call in with my boss tomorrow to ask if I can reduce my hours slightly on my civvy job and that would allow me to do escorting one day during the week. To do weekday calls for business clients who can just pop out of the office for an hour you know ... then I plan to basically do that for the next year, bank really hard and putting everything away to earn the maximum amount to buy an ISA.'

Sierra is explicit about her desire for class mobility:

'At the end of the day I just want to be middle class you know ... I just want security. I don't want to be rich rich, I just want to be sure that I don't have to worry from month to month about how I'm gonna pay the rent ... I do all these fucking ventures, and all this bullshit study ... just to get that middle-class bullshit heterosexual dream, but that's the reality unfortunately ... just to get a middle-class life and a family and be happy.'

Contributors talked a lot about the precarity of their jobs. Blu comments:

'It's all temporary, precarious, not stable and not long-term solutions, basically and that's kind of what my life has been like the last few years so at various points there's a lot more sex work at various points and then not nothing for quite a few weeks or a month or so, so I've gone between a lot of different kinds of jobs over the time.'

Blu's health issues complicate her employment situation and sex working:

'I wouldn't have gotten enough work to do it [sex work] full-time and pay my rent for a month ... I'm not willing to spend every waiting minute of my life on it and other people do well but their lives are all work and that's not what I want. I would rather have a little less money and be able to do stuff that I actually care about because I have health to think about, my energy reserves are a lot more stretched.'

Blu was unable to find any stable work after completing a degree and then ended up on benefits and was sanctioned after being outed to the government: "I'd been quite lucky but until the sanctions had them taken off me, but it was like I knew that I would get that money that I can count on. I would be able to pay my rent at least." Although some may criticise Blu for supplementing low benefits income with sex work, she did so after facing disability stigma in the jobs market:

'It's just so exhausting … and there are so many stigmas and not being able to make money is just so much work in a way that I didn't realise. We juggle so many different kinds of work in ways that people don't recognise it as work … there's not sick pay or holiday pay, so actually I would be happy to do it if there was stability of income but there's not. So, it's not the actual work it's everything else, so I guess my ideal thing would be a part time job maybe 3 days a week … enough to have a dignified quality of life.'

Although some contributors earned double or triple the national average income of £26,884 (as of May 2018), others teetered on a knife edge because their jobs in both sex work and square work were precarious. And if outed, contributors would lose status in both worlds and employment, and may lose family and friends. Sex industry work is still tainted and unstable. Sex work is sales, a saturated boom and bust industry without any wide-scale regulation or standardisation by the workers themselves around pricing, services or occupational health, especially in criminalised and quasi-legal policy environments, such as is found in the UK. Contributors could not rely upon a steady stream of clients in sex industries. Sierra quips: "They are unpredictable … they won't call for 6 months and then suddenly it's like 'hi how are you doing?'"

Franco expresses his frustration:

'financial fear and financial insecurity. It's like where is my next money coming from … it really pisses me off, people think you're an escort and you are rich. "You're charging a £100 or £250 an hour for escorting, you must be rich" and it's like if I was seeing 10 clients a week I would be, but it changes. And the insecurity of it that fills me with a lot of fear.'

Blu was not the only contributor who had to sign on due to lack of work prospects after completing an education. One anonymous contributor discussed how demeaning this was:

'I had nothing, and I was signing on and they treated you like absolute shit! It's like ridiculous, disgusting! You think you've done something good, you've done a PhD and you think you're a person and you're a customer or whatever, but they just have a way of demeaning you so easily and subtly. … they say "oh what's your post code you're in the wrong place" and then make you like go over a mile from [home] and it seems a bit arbitrary. They don't allow you to go the job centre closest to your home just to put you off … and they do things like randomly, they would say that they called me to tell me to come in and they hadn't, or they'd call and hang up. Or they would randomly tell me that I had to come in every day for no reason.'

This contributor joins others in the study who felt a loss of personhood after having to apply for benefits when they could not find work, even after achieving a doctorate, the highest level of education possible. What do we say to someone like this? They are willing and available to work, skilled and take on every job they can, but still fall short of money to live. What is on offer for these individuals, to prevent their involvement in sex industries or to support their transition from duality? They get stigma and criminalisation but no real support to earn income commensurate with their skills and experience. Victimising Blu because she defines sex work as work does not solve the underlying issue of underemployment and labour precarity.

The violence of exclusion

Based on all of this, should there not be an interest in hearing from sex workers in development of policies that affect their lives? That appears not to be the case. The voices of people in studies like these are often ignored because they disagree that it's the sex industry that oppresses them. They see beyond the specific industries and into broader marketplaces, the structure of our economies and the interests of those in power. It is here where they find the inequities that negatively affect their lives. They do not fit who is stereotypically defined as a sex worker. How are we going to rescue these contributors, who make more money than most and possess more education than the average UK worker? The façade that sex workers are all victims or that they need specific feminist lobby groups or ill-informed policies to save them from themselves falls apart in light of who trades sex today. Some sex workers are already working on issues that affect their well-being and clearly state that 'We are not waiting to be invited into the feminist movement. We have always been here' (Mac and Smith, 2018, p 220).

Some may argue that this book is about the most elite sex workers who are not representative of the industry. Incorrect. This book delivers insights from a couple of dozen working class sex workers, who, by all accounts, are typical of the bulk of the off-street sex industry. As noted in the Introduction, we do not know the precise make-up of off-street sex industries. There is research into online sex work; however, these studies tend to be based on small samples and can only provide snapshots into the lives of online sex workers. Sex is traded outside of these channels and in private networks as well. Sex workers who are willing to come forward and share their lives with us should be heard as they bring important insights about themselves and, in so doing, about us.

Contributors in this study felt exploited by work but not because their employment is found in sex industries, but due to labour precarity and the lack of recognition and understanding of their circumstances. They take issue with the silencing of their voices, analyses and contributions to understanding work and society. Nagle (1997) posits that non-sex working feminists produce discourses related to selling sex and exclude sex workers from the processes of their own representations. This is a lived reality among sex workers. Nagle urges an acknowledgement of the perspectives of sex working feminists who have been working to reduce exploitation within sex industries for decades. Contributors here are marginalised but not marginal. People living dual lives are not peripheral. These contributors are involved in far more economic activity in both mainstream and informal economies than many assume. They use income from dual occupations towards mainstream businesses, education, property investments, savings, to fund projects and to finance the all-important social mobility. They not only undergo the stresses of managing duality for themselves, they are doing this so that their children can start their lives debt free. True grit is demonstrated in Joy's motivation for duality. She raised £20,000 in nine weeks to pay for her child's tuition to ensure that they incurred no debt for an education and ended the cycle of poverty and student debt in her family for a generation. It is important that contributors like Joy are heard because the underlying financial challenges that they face are not atypical of others in the working classes and foreshadows a trend of people incorporating informal economy work due to financial hardship and economic drivers such as the COVID-19 pandemic and rising unemployment. Policy development in the areas of income support and labour protections could be more robust if informed by sex workers. Excluding them from defining social problems and collaborating across multi-agencies to seek solutions that directly affect their lives and livelihoods is a form of violence.

So too is sanctioning people like one contributor in this study for supplementing low benefits income with sex work for six months after she was outed. This policy decision serves no one. The contributor was subsequently driven to use dangerous methods in sex work to make money as the fact she was being sanctioned made her more reliant on sex work and she made compromises in the services she offered. She had to deprioritise her health and safety because she was desperate for money. She was 'sexiting' (Bowen, 2013) and had clear goals towards full-time employment; however, transitioning is not funded appropriately, and benefit levels were too low to gain traction for social mobility. This is legislated poverty.

We cannot claim to be seeking understanding of sex work, sex work 'exiting' and transitioning, the impacts of austerity, and labour trends among diverse populations of (marginalised) workers if we do not include the experiences of these contributors when crafting law and policy in housing, Universal Credit (UC) and other social investments in health and education. Testimony from sex workers, representatives from sex worker support organisations, and myself on behalf of National Ugly Mugs (NUM, 2019) confirmed that the switch over from other benefits into the catch-all benefits structure was ill-considered, leaving confusion and financial uncertainty for the most impoverished people in society in its wake. Some were left with less money after moving onto UC; the five-week wait guaranteed many would face poverty and be forced into survival work including the trading of sex for the first time. The inaccessibility of digitally facilitated benefits also led those who had previously 'exited' to return. The online application process was insensitive to those who were not computer literate and without access to stable or free internet. Furthermore, a former Department of Work and Pensions employee came forward to talk about how he trained staff members to get benefit applicants off the phone, the most accessible means to talk to the government, using a flowchart and a lot of apologies and deflections (Sky News, 2018). This is legislated poverty.

Some contributors to this study worked in roles in the public trust and they lived under a constant threat of being discovered. Roles in the public trust, including enforcement and security, health, social care, and education, require employees to take oaths. Some private sector roles in banking and finance may require similar commitments to good conduct. One anonymous contributor remarked that if her square job found out about her sex industry work they could fire her under existing policies:

> 'It would probably come under any clauses liable to bring the company into disrepute, which is the sort of catch all phrase … this allows you to get rid of people on the basis … like they've gone before the judge for drunk and disorderly and stuff like that. So, there is a threat there. I mean I'd fight it if they tried to get rid of me on that basis, because I'm not doing anything illegal you know. And I do take steps to try to keep a very clear demarcation between my two lives.'

Sex workers would likely be dismissed from their 'square' job contracts under clauses related to 'gross misconduct' and based on the code of conduct at their respective workplaces. What constitutes gross misconduct is not defined; however, under the Employment Rights Act (1996) dismissal must be reasonable and employees have the right not to be unfairly dismissed.[1] The Act does not set out or define the term 'gross misconduct' but cases have helped to clarify this. In *Dairy Produce Packers Ltd v Beverstock* [1981] IRLR 265, it was held that 'gross misconduct' included bringing an organisation into serious disrepute. The Advisory, Conciliation and Arbitration Service (ACAS) Code provides some insights into gross misconduct by listing examples such as physical violence and insubordination; however, misconduct may vary based on the type of business.[2]

A Sussex police constable was dismissed after signing off due to illness when it was discovered that he was doing sex work on the side to supplement sick benefits (Nagesh, 2016). Constables swear an oath in service to the Queen and work in the public trust. They are not in fact employees, but office holders who take an oath. The Police Code of Ethics requires that they, whether on duty or not, do nothing to undermine public trust.[3] In the case of the Sussex officer, he filed a complaint with the Independent Press Standards Organisation (IPSO) that was not upheld, after being outed for sex working by a journalist with a hidden camera who posed as a client.[4] His dismissal from the police service was lawful because 'police officers must behave in a manner that does not discredit the police service or undermine public confidence, whether on or off duty'.[5] Another officer from Sussex in 2018 resigned before being dismissed for gross misconduct after being caught selling sex via an ASW platform;[6] he was nonetheless found guilty.[7]

The argument here is not that police officers ought to be sex workers, although there is a well-established market for them. Nor is it about oaths. I have taken an oath to public service myself for a role I held in a provincial government in Canada. People who take oaths must uphold them as a sacred duty. The issue here, from a perspective of designing out vulnerabilities to survival sex, is that if even our police officers trade sex as a side hustle, it is less about the behaviour of any one person, and more about the structures and contexts within which those decisions are made. If we do not seek to understand the choice architecture, how then can we develop standards that protect us from having to make the harshest decisions to survive? How are we held accountable for how we treat people who trade sex? Is this 'responsibilising' individuals just part of the design in the neoliberal context?

Here is a little context. In 2017 pay scales for constables ranged between £19,971 and £38,382 after seven years of service.[8] Sussex police constables on sick leave may earn half pay[9] for a series of weeks, equating to a gross sick income of between £10,000 and £20,000 per annum. Furthermore, the median rent in the South-East in 2016 was the second highest in the country at £850/month or £10,200 per year.[10]

It is well documented that people with disabilities do sex work due to the income and flexibility it offers. For example, Blu's health issues affected her ability to work full time in any career:

'I haven't been able to do it [sex work] full-time and not even enough work to pay my rent for a month so really, it's always been very much a part time thing. I think that's because I'm not willing to spend every waking minute of my life on it and other people do well, but their lives are all work and that's not what I want … because I have health to think about, my energy reserves are a lot more stretched than most people.'

We must ask what it is about sick benefits and our statutory sick pay (SSP) that leaves ill and disabled people struggling to make ends meet. This is legislated poverty.

There are contributors to this study who are health care providers. Nurses, similar to police officers and doctors, are in the public trust and take an oath called the Nightingale Pledge. This pledge has undergone many incarnations; however, the 1893 version required nurses to swear before God to live in 'purity' and 'abstain from whatever is deleterious and mischievous'.[11] Although later versions of this pledge are argued to be problematic (Adams, 2019), there is no doubt that the sentiments about purity remain and doing sex work alongside nursing, although the core features may be integrative, would be seen as a violation of the public trust. According to the 2018 Nursing and Midwifery Council's Code, sections 20.3 and 20.4, to uphold trust, nurses are expected to have an awareness of their behaviour and its impacts as well as being law abiding (NMC, 2015). Contributors who work in education are also expected to uphold the reputations of their respective universities, and these institutions have discretion in determining what constitutes misconduct. Contributors worried about the lack of policy protections if they were outed at work and lost employment due to stigma and discrimination for past and concurrent sex work. While gross misconduct *tends* to relate to conduct while someone is working, if they are working in roles in the public trust, sex working could be considered to be gross misconduct. Even though working in sex industries is not illegal, employers can argue that it will bring their company into disrepute, particularly if employees sign contracts to this effect. Active sex workers can be harmed by workplace policies that take a moralistic view on sex work and deem those who do it unfit, irrespective of why they are doing sex work, what work they are doing, and how they are doing it. This is legislated poverty.

What is it about all forms of sex industry work that make participating in any form of it a violation of public trust? What is it about commercialising contact and non-contact intimacy that makes the people doing it unworthy of public trust? Ironically, in Jamaican culture, sex workers are called *night nurses*. Sex workers cite trust as something that they must establish in order to provide services. Recalling Mary's comments:

'I can make people feel comfortable very quickly … but I mean like definitely like when a lot of clients are nervous, like they're only going to be here for an hour so you've got 15 minutes to get them to feel comfortable enough to

get all their clothes off, have sex and cum … there's a lot
of skills that you use in sex work.'

We have to ask ourselves who benefits from the exclusion of sex
workers in influencing workplace policies, UC or from their helping us
understand the financial pressures that they experience? Who stands to
gain from the denial of their 'worker' status? They have little protection
in square jobs if they are outed as former sex workers. There are no
protections found under sections 13, 14 or 19 of the 2010 Equality
Act. Sex workers are not protected in sex industry jobs either because
of the quasi-legal status of sex workers in the UK (Allaboutlaw.co.uk,
2020), which effectively blocks employment protections and access to
anti-exploitation and anti-discrimination law and regulation policies.
What is our end game?

This chapter asks more questions than it answers. There are several
conversations that can be had to openly discuss alienation, work and
workplace policies as they affect people who trade sex. There is also
an opportunity to discuss how we take care of workers, and each other
when we get ill. Can SSP be increased so that workers who are sick
temporarily do not also have to worry about how they are going to
survive and pay their bills alongside any illnesses so that people are not
forced into survival sex? Currently, we offer £94.25 per week in SSP
if someone is sick for four days in a row (excluding the self-employed)
for those who earn at least £118 per week. Those on zero-hours
contracts tend not to meet this minimum requirement nor are those 16
to 24 years of age or over 65 (TUC, 2020). The UK Health Minister,
Matt Hancock, admitted on the BBC's *Question Time* that he could not
live on SSP at the current rate (Carmichael, 2020). We have choices
to make about if and how we protect the young, the old, the ill and
the impoverished. We can choose to better invest our resources and
provide adequate social supports.

7

"Don't judge us as different from you": Wyatt

This short chapter will summarise the major themes presented in this book and some issues that arose for contributors as they pertain to representation and power. The chapter will be split into two sections that will discuss the arising concerns under headings: 'If sex workers were in control' and 'If sex workers were really treated as victims'. The book ends with a brief summary of major contributions and aims for future research.

If sex workers were in control

Sex workers are diverse as we see here, and a single label or moniker masks (deliberately or otherwise) who really trades sex. Those who stand to gain from the mischaracterisation of sex workers and their industries benefit from ensuring that workers have little political power and no means to gain control over the industries that they work within. Keeping industry workers from enjoying the benefits of labour rights in the UK means that for many, their work will always be mediated by third parties, some of whom, but not all, are dangerous extortionists. We must acknowledge that there is work in exploitation and exploitation in work across all industries. Supporting sex industry workers in continuing to unionise and to self-regulate, as well as in setting policy and standards is critical for the future. This is crime prevention by environmental design, where sex workers can eliminate the conditions, roles and practices that cause them harm. The sex industry as a service industry will shift from being wholly a client and third party-driven industry to one with a more cooperative flavour, where workers' rights are part of the ethos.

We can begin first by acknowledging that for the vast majority, sex work is work.

'Sex work is just as valid and valued a work as any other square work that people do. And it is as varied and diverse as square work, different forms of square work and basically we're no different. You know, I think that's what I would want to convey like you know, *don't judge us as different from you*.' (Wyatt)

Existing law, such as the brothel-keeping legislation, section 33A of the Sexual Offences Act 2003, are harmful because they negatively affect sex workers. This legislation forces off-street workers, to work in isolation instead of with others who are lateral to them in role. Dangerous people target sex workers due to a range of vulnerabilities that include those caused by legislative 'tunnel vision', stigma and discrimination. Also, for many, there is no in-person contact with clients; however, there are opportunities for harm through cybercrime and other means. Sex workers from all locations within the array of industries can experience harm, forced labour and survival sex. We must partner with sex workers from across the diverse businesses and industries to create guiding principles, occupational health and safety standards, and policies and standard operating procedures (SOPs) that ensure fair and appropriate treatment of these workers in relevant contexts. There is no shortage of sex workers, scholars and practitioners who can support this effort.

Sex worker input into the structure and regulation of third parties is a priority. There are those that position sex workers as their product, and those who view sex workers as their customers. Between these two approaches to managing sex work businesses, whether they are proprietary or incorporated, there are vast differences in how sex workers are treated. Although this is beyond the scope of this book, it falls in line with how contributors manage sex work and the risks posed by third parties who have information about their involvement in sex industries and the power they wield as a result. Brouwers and Herrmann (2020), for example, discuss the influential role ASWs have on the economic and financial well-being of sex workers during the COVID-19 pandemic and the role of these businesses in providing support.

Sex workers and those who support their labour rights, safety at work and access to healthcare speak out against sex worker exclusionary radical feminism (Miano, 2017) that sidelines sex workers who professionalise their work and reject victim narratives. Those who want equitable access to labour rights and entitlements, and the support to move in and out of sex work with impunity, need to be fully engaged in discursive practice, in the Foucauldian sense, and formal processes of meaning-making about sex industries and their regulation. If sex workers were in control, there would be no need for religious factions, politicians and proponents of some feminisms to speak out instead of active sex workers, nor would policy decisions be made from the perspectives of people who, although passionate, are neither active in sex industries nor researchers in this field.

It is time to progress from antiquated moralistic approaches to sex work in our society. I am aware that some do not want a safe sex industry and are happy for sex workers to suffer collateral damage so long as they eradicate the purchase and sale of sex. Sex workers are not sinners. Associating sex workers and exit projects to Mary Magdalene is inaccurate, and so too is the labelling of this woman, who dared to have her own gospel, a prostitute,[1] but I digress. Sex work is not a character flaw, nor is it illegal. It is done in response to a variety of push and pull factors, including poverty, precarity and the inequitable distribution of resources, wealth and possibilities. It is also time to call out representations that are not driven by or heavily shaped by active sex workers. There are few marginalised populations in our society that have resources provided to charities and state services for their support and care, that do not have members of the respective populations employed or in governance. We would question a women's organisation that had no women involved or a group serving people with accessibility issues that only employed able-bodied individuals. We would take issue with (mis)representation in these cases. We should require the same for those who design policy or provide services to sex workers.

If sex workers were really treated as victims

We have advanced a little from sex workers as sinners to criminals to deviants and we are plodding along towards labelling them as victims. Although these are not clear stages, nor do I imply that this is the best way forward, there are noticeable shifts in rhetoric. Unfortunately, many sex workers still experience criminal sanctions and suffer from a range of enforcement tactics that influence their lives in negative ways such as fines, incarceration and deportation.

Sex workers are not wholly victims but are meant to be treated as such within frameworks that define sex work as harm. Victimhood is conditionally bestowed upon those who fit ideal victim stereotypes and co-sign narratives that reduce negative outcomes such as stigma and aid in avoiding state violence in the form of deportation and criminalisation. Sex workers are often victimised by *other people* and forced to escape dangers caused by those who take advantage of their trust and vulnerabilities. We must work to end this harm. The victim/survivor narrative as it applies to some sex workers carries with it a 'recovery' capital not available to those who do not fit the characteristics of ideal victims because they are otherwise considered dangerous based on race and cultural heritage, citizenship, poverty and addictions, non-conforming gender-performances and divergence from heteronormativity. Those who define their sex work as work, as these contributors do for example, and reject victimhood as constructed by outsiders, highlight how they are harmed by systemic biases, discriminatory policies and power structures such as capitalism. These structures, as explicated by relationalists, are in fact *other people* and social forms. Far from being victims, sex workers who hold the view that labour relations, policy and market structures contribute to their vulnerability are likely pathologised, deemed 'deviant', criminal and service resistant. Having a labour analysis informed by lived experience in sex work is penalised through social exclusion. Scoular and O'Neill (2007) exposed the practice of the social exclusion and the 'punitiveness' of policies aimed at ameliorating harms against sex workers through the enterprise of progressive government and a not-so-new governance strategy for prostitution. Renewed strategies derived from the 2004 Home Office consultation document *Paying the Price*, according to these researchers, only yielded old and familiar responsiblisation of sex workers and forced welfarism through multi-agency strategies. Contributors heard from in this book live under the constant fear of being outed and the silencing and exclusion that follows because they will be made into public spectacles by media and others, and there will be no attention paid to contemporary antagonisms and the sources of their oppression. Sex workers will suffer from the unmet promises of support to women who trade sex and the harmful power structures and social conditions that we are all complicit in reproducing.

We cannot simultaneously disenfranchise sex workers as 'victims' in need of rescue and also deny that they are 'workers' in need of labour rights. So, which is it? Both? Neither? They are not given the space to define what they need because those with the power to silence them do just that, as we see with Umbrella Lane and SWAI who wanted to access COVID-19 emergency funding for their large memberships. Sex workers are suffering and left to starve because of these political games. This is unethical. The 'fugazi' victimhood that we bestow upon sex workers cannot shield them against discriminatory employment policies and heavy-handed enforcement initiatives that put their lives at risk. If sex workers were really treated as victims, the (2020) 'Code of Practice for Victims of Crime in England and Wales'[2] would fully apply to their lives and circumstances, and all who victimise them would be subject to sanctions.

If sex workers were really treated as victims (of poverty, exploitation or circumstance) it would be illegal to stigmatise them and unethical to fire them from the square jobs that they hold because this would compromise their economic security and force them into dangerous ways of working in mainstream and informal economies. Worse, they could become unemployable full stop, and thus dependent on the state for survival indefinitely. Not to mention the toll stigma and unemployment has on (mental) health and well-being. Some sex workers, after being outed, are driven to drug misuse or suicide as the weight of social stigma and the impact of the public gaze intruding into their private lives, along with the struggle to make money to survive, all become too much to bear. A woman who was to take part in the research that informs this book was outed as a sex worker. She was subject to public ridicule, suffered from high levels of stress and a loss of earnings. She resisted and spoke out against injustice and hypocrisy for as long as she could, but ultimately took her own life.

If sex workers were really treated as victims, we would fully commit to the safety of active sex workers and enact anti-discrimination policies. Beyond hate crime initiatives, of which sex workers should lead the interrogation, occupation ought to be explored as a protected element within labour rights for those discriminated against in tainted jobs. People who live dual lives and those who work in 'dirty' jobs may experience any combination of the three taints (physical, social and moral) – this in addition to the rare Jekyll and Hyde dualism (Ashforth et al, 2000) and the psychological harms associated with role transitioning. Hate crime approaches may assume that 'sex worker' is a category of identity. According to the Crown Prosecution Service (2017), hate crimes are committed against those possessing protected characteristics (race, religion, sexual orientation, transgender identity and disability) that may be constructed as elements of identity.[3] As we see here and in other research about sex workers, for many, sex work is what they do, not who they are. Contributors strongly challenged the idea of being forced to identify with work or sex work in this respect because they have little control over what it means to be a sex worker in our society. A larger debate on this topic is necessary and many look forward to participating in it.

If sex workers were really treated as victims it would also be illegal to evict them from premises, as occurred to an anonymous contributor to this book. We would not criminalise them, shame or displace them and we would operate with a deeper understanding of why they trade sex and how to support those who desire transition to other work. We would not get away with divestment and inadequately addressing the economic drivers and other factors that contribute to their involvement. We would be accountable to the design of transition supports with sex workers and establish determinants for success that are evaluated against a theory of change and key performance indicators (KPIs) that they help construct. For example, researchers who led the evaluation of the Managed Area in Leeds released their independent evaluation in July 2020 in which 'exiting' women from sex work was a deliverable. The

Managed Area was proven to be a tremendous success as a safety strategy and as a means to support active street-based workers; however, due to the complexity of transitioning they removed 'exiting' as a performance measure (Roach et al, 2020). We have to find ways to measure 'exit' in programmes that we fund to achieve this aim. Interpreting sex work as harm is not a precursor to supporting transition. Investing in initiatives that hold a more neutral harm reduction stance on sex work or that recognise that sex work is work are worthy of investment for transition support. We must fully invest in a range of transition supports that get resources to people to fund the changes they want to see in their lives. These can be evaluated upon established KPIs. Without this, 'exiting' will continue to be characterised in ways that suit political agendas, and sex workers who want to leave the industry will be forced to do so without the necessary resources.

If sex workers were really treated as victims, everyone would know that 184 members of that community were murdered in the UK since we started counting in the 1990s. We would not need the High Court to overturn policies such as section 222 in Hull. It would not have been revived in 2014 in the first place. Sex workers and those living dual lives have always been with us. They have always been part of our families, neighbourhoods and workforces. It is time for all of us to make decisions about how we are going to treat them and have full transparency about this. If they are victims, then comfort them in the ways that we know how. By giving them room to speak from their experiences, inform our responses and receive full social and legal protection. If they are deviant criminals then be open about this positioning and justify their treatment through moralities, religions and feminisms, but prepare for these ideologies to be challenged and brought before judges to weigh facts and act in the interests of the most vulnerable. We have seen judges review 'prostitution' laws in Canada, for example the *Canada (AG) v Bedford* 2013 SCC 72 case that struck down sections 210 Keeping or being found in a common bawdy house (repealed 19 September 2019 (Bill C-75), 212(1)(j) Procuring and Living on the avails of prostitution (Repealed 6 December 2014) and 213(1)(c) Communicating in Public for the purpose of prostitution. In this case, the Supreme Court of Canada voted unanimously to overturn these specific sections of Canadian law that violated the Canadian Charter of Rights and Freedoms, sections 1, 2 and 7, as they relate to freedoms of expression and communication, as well as life, liberty and security of person. For the first time, in law, the lives of sex workers were valued and elevated above property or any harms associated with 'public nuisance'. The displacement, stigmatisation and crimiminalisation of sex workers was deemed unconstitutional.

If sex workers were really treated as victims, we would decouple enforcement from support for migrant sex workers. Workers of colour and migrants receive the most police contact, sit at the lowest rungs of the whorearchy and are victims of xenophobia, hate crime and other forms of victimisation by those who seek to harm the vulnerable in our communities. Police policies, such as referring migrant sex workers to immigration, as lawyer Wendy Lyon pointed out, are employed in the Republic of Ireland. The ECP 2019 report on Brexit documents this practice in the UK as well. Experts in applied ethics need to evaluate enforcement strategies and weigh criminal justice outcomes against the suffering experienced by these victims and the conditions that perpetuate their vulnerability. Migrant sex workers experience crime and do not report it because we do not provide victim support to them. I hope our aim is to rid our societies of dangerous people and not to further harm victims because perpetrators do not need any more help to do that.

We as a community of sex workers, researchers and professionals representing multi-agency interests, can work together to develop robust policies with a greater understanding of the landscape of cause and effect in the lives of sex workers. We can shape initiatives under some core remits for health and safety, access to resources, representation and rights, but be we have be honest about the positioning and treatment of sex workers across our institutions and the implications of mischaracterisations and exclusionary politics. Sex workers exist beyond reductionist labels of 'victim' or 'deviant'. Those who gain from the chaos that inadequate policies and harmful legislation create in the lives of sex workers are well served by some of the loudest prohibitionist anti-sex work advocates with the power to decide who gets heard from and how resources are distributed. Keeping active sex workers from having any influence in policy decisions guarantees that nothing will be devised with their 'true interests' in mind.

Protection

Banking on change

There are negative outcomes to pretending to treat sex workers as victims that block their access to the tools and resources needed for security and emancipation. At times, sex workers are treated as criminals when they try to access financial instruments and open bank accounts with their legally earned incomes. Many sole sex workers hide the fact that they are doing sex work because banks have refused to let sex workers open accounts. NUM case workers received calls from sex workers who had this experience beginning in the spring of 2020. Contributors in this book hold square jobs and have bank accounts but worry about saving or investing more money than they have earned on paper or having assets taken away from them. It is unclear whether some banks see sex workers' money as proceeds of crime or if they have adopted a blanket response based on some trafficking discourses that conflate sex workers and trafficking victims. Even so, preventing any victim from opening an account in their own name as a pathway to independence is counterproductive. It would be like denying a victim of domestic violence a bank account. It is also hypocritical, given that banks have no problem storing and investing monies from corporations that overprice goods and services while underpaying workers and evading taxes. The 'fugazi' victimhood bestowed on sex workers does not carry enough social/cultural capital to get a person a bank account. What is worse, the banks that do this are denying workers access to legal ways of storing and managing their money, in an environment, due to COVID-19, that prefers consumers to use bank cards instead of cash.[4] Furthermore, a major barrier to transitioning from sex industries (for those who choose to and can plan for it) is having the money to move, pay security deposits and start jobs. Sex workers and contributors engage in sexiting 'because change costs money' (Bowen, 2015, p 442). Financial exclusion contributes to the marginalisation and disenfranchisement of sex workers and is an (unintended) consequence of the victim narrative.

Police protection

Sex workers are disincentivised to report the harms they experience to police. Many report that raids, deportation, increased monitoring and criminalisation have a chilling effect and are deterrents to involving police in their lives. There have been incidents where money, phones and laptops have been taken or confiscated by police officers and not returned or returned after groups like ECP, NUM and others, including officials, wrote to prosecutors to explain the circumstances and implications.[5] These kinds of negative interactions remain in the forefront of one's mind when contemplating police involvement.

Since duality occurs among hidden off-street sex workers, although they may otherwise have access to police and may have had positive encounters as expected among the sample demographic, when they are engaging in sex industry work, the option of police protection all but disappears. Contributors risk being outed as sex workers in their personal lives and to associates in their square jobs as well. Many contributors and sex workers are also students and have children and the same obligations as anyone else around family and careers. Recall Juno's remark: "... a lot of sex workers are not out or are in vulnerable situations. They can't you know go to police."

When crimes against sex workers go unreported or underreported, our national statistics fail to provide an accurate picture of criminality and we under-resource strategies that can reduce these harms. The 'dark figure' in criminology refers to underreported crime and was first coined by Belgian mathematician and sociologist Adolphe Quetelet in 1832 (Penney 2013). Organisations, such as the one that I am responsible for, NUM, provide a mechanism for active sex workers from across industries to report harm and receive victim-centred support in accessing legal measures for remedy, through the state, such as the police and courts, along with other resources found in the community. Reports of harm to sex workers are converted to warnings and sent to others in the industry to inform their decisions about who they choose to see as clients. These warnings help prevent crime and are, with the consent of the victim, provided to intelligence agencies to help protect our entire society. The data and insights arising from these reports inform NUM victim services, community education and systemic advocacy. NUM received almost 1,000 reports in 2019 and only 9 per cent of off-street workers consented to involve the police in investigating crimes against them.[6] This is down from roughly 30 per cent in 2012. Individuals who target sex workers are particularly despicable because they do so with the awareness that sex workers have few rights, are often not believed as witnesses of their own experiences and are treated as disposable. When sex workers become victims of crime and are not able to access police, like the contributors here, it is a failing of victim supports and a systemic problem for all of us.

There have been some strides taken by police to acknowledge the diversity of sex industry workers and the differing policing approaches needed to tackle exploitation. Viewing all sex workers as victims and subjecting them to prohibition and indirect criminalisation is problematic. Efforts are made by practitioner groups and researchers to share knowledge with police as done through community education at NUM, research such as the Beyond the Gaze project,[7] and training provided by other community groups. NUM, for example, contributed to the National Police Chiefs' Council (NPCC) 'National Policing Sex Work and Prostitution Guidance' (2019),[8] which suggests that police not make moral judgements about sex workers or treat them like criminals, but instead evaluate the differing contexts and situations that sex workers operate within in order to devise appropriate responses. I use the term 'suggests' deliberately because the NPCC document is guidance and not a national police policy operationalised across all forces.

There are bound to be challenges in establishing a standardised police response to sex working victims given that we have 43 police forces, but we sorely need one. Sex workers comprise an intersectional group that includes impoverished, working class and elite populations of all backgrounds, as well as these contributors who live dual lives but are otherwise part of the mainstream workforce. Among people who trade sex, there is a general mistrust of police, in part because of how they perceive sex workers as being treated; their lived experiences of police (biographies, history) as unpredictable or negative; their vicarious exposures to police enforcement upon sex workers; and media representations of sex workers as problematic and police operations towards them as necessary and just. Sex workers and contributors here weigh the benefits and risks of reporting to any resource – police and NUM included. It is a simple cost benefit analysis. If reporting the harm that they experience 'costs' sex workers more in terms of personal and professional status, and benefits with respect to justice, support and protections for them and their communities, then they will not report and we will continue to see under-engagement with police by sex workers. Sex workers will, however, report crime to organisations that provide supports and add value to their lives. We cannot advocate for victim-centred support and then, through legislation and practice, actively produce more victims or remain inaccessible to people who need protection. We in the UK can do better.

Serving sex workers

There is a distinction to be made between sex worker-serving and sex worker-led organisations, where the former have (charitable) aims towards improving well-being, rights or some aspect of sex workers' lives, and the latter are groups where sex workers are involved in all levels of the organisation in impactful ways. Most sex worker support organisations in the UK are of the former variety and as such are at a disadvantage if investment from sex workers is lacking. The ultimate recommendation for practitioner organisations who depend on insights from diverse on- and off-street populations of sex workers to shape their services is to hire active and former sex workers as lateral and fully empowered members of staff. Avoid, if at all possible, hiring sex workers in symbolic roles as 'peer' workers, who have no real power to shape and influence the organisation. Organisations with sex workers on the staff can then create working cultures and policies where lived experiences are valued. Organisations that purport to serve sex workers must employ them and we can no longer invest in groups that choose not to do so. We have challenges to face around stigma and tokenistic involvement of sex workers but policies of preferential hiring of people in and from the sex industries and establishing meaningful partnerships with sex working communities are important steps for sex worker-serving organisations and strategic investors.

Hester et al (2019) state that charities have 'real time' access to trends in sex industries; however, practitioners have a distance to go in terms of supporting hidden populations of sex workers. Many front-facing services cater to the most visible populations of sex workers, who at times approach charities for support with poverty, homelessness and health issues. These workers risk being outed if they are seen visiting bricks and mortar locations known for servicing sex workers. Further risks may be posed by how records are kept or the disclosure of information between practitioner types in health services and adult care and government. In order for services to be safe to use for those living dual lives and others who must remain discreet, anonymised ways of accessing must be established. Some organisations are exploring this now with respect to inclusion health services for marginalised populations. For face-to-face services, this could mean having discreet VIP-type access to buildings, the use of passwords and pseudonyms and codes to associate people with files and to have explicit standards around the collection and management of information about sex work/sex workers.

Similarly, for organisations that provide digital support, anonymity can be built into technologies such as phone lines, online chat, conferencing, text-based support, surveys and so on. Engagement strategies must run alongside the uptake and operationalisation of anti-stigma and anti-oppression education created by sex workers, which inform the policies and practices of the charitable organisations, health services and adult care. Hester et al, (2019) recommend uniformity around the data collection done by charities that work with sex workers. Although some have goals for this information to be provided to the state there is some merit to capturing a deeper understanding of demographics for programming and advocacy within the third sector for the benefit of sex workers. Community-based research on sex industries must be participant driven (Bowen and O'Doherty, 2014) where active sex workers partner in shaping the research agenda based on their priorities towards safety, health and inclusion.

Finally, representation matters. How sex workers are portrayed on charity websites, and content that is explicit versus that which is implicit, can be the difference between whether sex workers and these contributors access the service or not. Sex workers investigate the political positions and funding sources of charities as well as obtaining information from their networks, when deciding which services to use. Language such as 'service resistant' or 'chaotic lives', even 'complex needs', can be interpreted as derogatory and unfortunately used to characterise sex workers who avoid engaging with entities as a result of their needs for privacy or self-preservation. Some sex workers are managing dynamic and challenging life circumstances in contexts that are beyond their control, but this does not mean that they are chaotic, needy or resistant as a rule. Sex workers are resistant to poor treatment, to initiatives led by those they do not trust, that are designed without them or those that are of no material benefit to them.

Postscript

This book offers insights about both sex *as* work, and sex work *and* work that include the Continuum of SIWSQ Involvement, the Dual-life Relational Paradigm and the UK whorearchy. The Continuum of SIWSQ Involvement is a framework to situate the practices of people who blend sex work and square work and a way of talking about human behaviour in this context in ways that were not seen in some research about 'exiting' and in some analyses of UK labour markets. Although the practices of blending sex work with other jobs exists throughout history and across cultures, 'Duality' is a nascent concept and needs some further development as to its value in describing contemporary populations who work this way. Furthermore, the Continuum of SIWSQ Involvement can be expanded or contracted as we learn more about the practices of duality and how the people who work this way choose to have their activities represented.

The Dual-life Relational Paradigm is represented within a rudimentary Venn diagram that describes the complex fields that contributors operate within and containing their on- and offline trans-actions and relations. There may be some diversity in how these fields overlap, and how performances and audiences are managed, and even how the Continuum of SIWSQ Involvement is situated within this paradigm. Similarly, the UK whorearchy as it unfolded for these contributors may be only a starting place, to fully understand stratification within sex industries as co-constructive and co-dependent upon the ordering and valuing of bodies in mainstream societies.

All of these contributions and themes require targeted study. The original research '*In Plain Sight: An examination of 'duality', the simultaneous involvement in sex work and square work*' (2018) was exploratory in nature.[1] Insights from this work can inform a more complex mixed-methods study involving a much larger sample now that there is some clarity around what themes to investigate. The lived experiences of those who live dual lives are reflective of the values and conditions that exist in mainstream society. Survival sex/forced labour, poverty, racism, sexism are all the by-products of our priorities. If we do not like what we see reflected back to us in the stories of these contributors, we do not set about destroying the mirror, we change ourselves and thus our society from within. We restructure our core values and markets to be equitable, as equality is a myth and clearly a low bar. We deal with the present realities around labour markets, work and opportunities, and how our values and practices construct fields of striving, of potentialities, capitals and shape what is possible.

We need to end hypocrisies associated with sex work and the people who do it. We cannot say that sex work is inherently violent if that runs counter to their lived experiences of it. We cannot criminalise the purchase of sexual services and then provide no investment towards career change. We cannot drive sex workers out of our neighbourhoods and fine them as a way to protect them. We cannot pretend that our current policies and enforcement tactics keep sex workers safe. We cannot perpetuate the lie that we take a 'victim-centred approach' if sex workers do not enjoy the same protections as any other victim and must risk being outed and compromise their futures in order to engage with the state and access public and community services. Finally, with respect to how our tax dollars are spent, there must be more resources put towards prevention, intervention and stabilisation for populations that face structural inequity, stigma and victimisation. This would reduce costs associated with enforcement, the NHS and institutionalisation. The suffering that exists in our communities is of our own making. People who live dual lives are a product of our marketplace. We can no longer perpetuate the lie that hard work in square jobs alone brings success and staves off poverty.

To contributors

I opened this book warning others not to look for you ... I close it with a message to you. Stay hidden! Use your networks to find support and a sense of community because many people work the way you do. If you need to reach out to services, access the ones that are delivered with and for sex workers, that contain ways that you can be anonymous or truly control what information others know about you. Take part in studies about duality and sex industries that have undergone ethics approval, are worker-led or participatory and those that commit not to publicise the strategies you use to stay safe and alive. Find safe ways to influence your environment, to be heard and seen.

I deeply understand that child poverty is parent poverty. Keep hustling and being there for your children and families in ways that nothing or no one else is at this point in time.

My aim in writing this book is to insert your experiences into the public domain in a safe way that can guarantee that the insights you had the courage to share can no longer be invisibilised in research on transitioning, in advocacy and in the delivery of public and communities support services. Importantly, your lived experiences contribute to representations of our marketplaces and the process of precarisation. The ways you manage information, audiences and technologies, in addition to the elements of duality that challenge you, are interdisciplinary and will bring greater understanding to what we know about ourselves and our worlds of work. In my professional role, I commit to co-creating safety with you and all sex workers and making space for your populations to speak out and do for yourselves. Thankfully, there are many who share this aim and who choose to meet you in that transcendent field, beyond rightdoing and wrongdoing.

Notes

Introduction

1 https://equanimitysite.wordpress.com/2012/12/15/rumi-out-beyond-the-ideas/
2 See https://en.oxforddictionaries.com/definition/duality
3 See Zoroastrian Heritage http://zoroastrianheritage.blogspot.co.uk/2011/09/dual-duality-dualism-definitions.html
4 'Statement from Umbrella Lane on Covid-19 Response from Scottish Government' https://uglymugs.org/um/a-statement-from-umbrella-lane-on-covid-19-response-from-the-scottish-government
5 Save Our Eyes, Leeds http://saveoureyes.co.uk/
6 https://www.hulldailymail.co.uk/news/hull-east-yorkshire-news/councillor-prostitute-sex-election-leaflet-3609958
7 Central Statistics Office, 'Women and Men in Ireland 2019' https://www.cso.ie/en/releasesandpublications/ep/p-wamii/womenandmeninireland2019/genderequality/
8 Sex Work Research Hub, Student Sex Work Toolkit for Staff in Higher Education https://www.swrh.co.uk/blog/student-sex-work-toolkit-for-staff-in-higher-education
9 The Chronicle of Higher Learning (6 May 2018) 'Are you in a BS job in academe, you're hardly alone' https://www.chronicle.com/article/Are-You-in-a-BS-Job-In/243318?cid=FEATUREDNAV
10 The Guardian USA (28 September, 2017) 'Facing poverty, academics turn to sex work and sleeping in cars' https://www.theguardian.com/us-news/2017/sep/28/adjunct-professors-homeless-sex-work-academia-poverty

Chapter 1

1 See Feminist Current, 'Survivors say the Nordic model is our only hope' (15 March 2016) https://www.feministcurrent.com/2016/03/15/survivors-say-the-nordic-model-is-our-only-hope/
2 The Equality Trust (2019) 'Billionaire Britain' https://www.equalitytrust.org.uk/sites/default/files/news/attachments/Billionnaire%20Britain%20REPORT%20FINAL.pdf
3 Office for National Statistics https://www.ons.gov.uk/peoplepopulationandcommunity/personalandhouseholdfinances/incomeandwealth/bulletins/nowcastinghouseholdincomeintheuk/financialyearending2017#trends-in-household-incomes
4 Office for National Statistics https://www.gov.uk/national-minimum-wage-rates
5 Office for National Statistics https://www.ons.gov.uk/peoplepopulationandcommunity/personalandhouseholdfinances/incomeandwealth/bulletins/wealthingreatbritainwave5/2014to2016/previous/v1/pdf
6 Office for National Statistics https://www.ons.gov.uk/peoplepopulationandcommunity/personalandhouseholdfinances/debt/articles/householddebtinequalities/2016-04-04#individual-characteristics

Chapter 2

[1] Möbius strip https://en.wikipedia.org/wiki/M%C3%B6bius_strip

Chapter 3

[1] GDPR Information Portal EU https://gdpr-info.eu/
[2] Wired http://www.wired.co.uk/article/what-is-gdpr-uk-eu-legislation-compliance-summary-fines-2018
[3] https://www.gov.uk/data-protection
[4] https://www.gov.uk/government/collections/investigatory-powers-bill
[5] http://www.legislation.gov.uk/ukpga/2015/6/contents/enacted
[6] http://www.legislation.gov.uk/ukpga/2015/6/section/21/enacted
[7] Recently enacted HR s 1865 Fight Online Sex Trafficking Act 2017 (FOSTA) https://www.congress.gov/bill/115th-congress/house-bill/1865 and Senate s 1683 Bill Stop Enabling Sex Traffickers Act (SESTA) https://www.congress.gov/bill/115th-congress/senate-bill/1693 have resulted in online venues pulling personal ads and eliminating ad spaces that sex workers use to meet and screen their clients.
[8] Violence Against Sex Trade Workers in the DTES, 'Our Friday at Burnaby Campus', blog post 26 July 2009 https://vio493.wordpress.com/tag/cell-phones/
[9] 'Edward Snowden: American Intelligence Contractor', *Encyclopaedia Britannica* https://www.britannica.com/biography/Edward-Snowden
[10] Refers to 'Grey Man', to act inconspicuously in modern colloquialism. See https://www.urbandictionary.com/define.php?term=The%20Grey%20Man
[11] https://switter.at/about

Chapter 4

[1] *The Guardian*, 'Pound slumps to 31-year low following Brexit vote' https://www.theguardian.com/business/2016/jun/23/british-pound-given-boost-by-projected-remain-win-in-eu-referendum
[2] http://www.ibtimes.co.uk/number-hate-crimes-uk-have-surged-since-eu-referendum-1580245
[3] Scottish Independence Referendum http://scotlandreferendum.info/
[4] Translators note that 'prostitute' does not translate well from German and was not emphasising money for sex, but promiscuity. See Footnote 1, [SEK163a1] 'A Special Type of Choice of Object Made by Men (Contributions to the Psychology of Love I)', The Standard Edition of the Complete Psychological Works of Sigmund Freud, Volume XI (1910): Five Lectures on Psycho-Analysis, Leonardo da Vinci and Other Works, 163–76 https://icpla.edu/wp-content/uploads/2012/10/Freud-S.-1910.-A-Special-Type-of-Choice-of-Object-made-by-Men-Contributions-to-the-Psychology-of-Love-I-Volume-XI-1910-163-176..pdf
[5] Magdalena Group: 'How will Brexit affect the sex work industry?' blog post http://magdalenegroup.org/doorwayblog/how-will-brexit-affect-the-sex-work-industry/ was accessed July 2017 and no longer available as of October 2020.
[6] *Irish Legal News* (25 August 2020) 'Migrants assisting criminal investigations referred to GNIB as a matter of policy' https://irishlegal.com/article/migrants-assisting-criminal-investigations-referred-to-gnib-as-matter-of-policy

Chapter 6

[1] Employment Rights Act 1996, ss 94 and 96.

² ACAS Code, paragraph 24 https://www.acas.org.uk/acas-code-of-practice-for-disciplinary-and-grievance-procedures/html#discipline:-keys-to-handling-disciplinary-issues-in-the-workplace
³ College of Policing, *Code of Ethics: A Code of Practice for the Principles and Standards of Professional Behaviour for the Policing Profession of England and Wales*, July 2014 (Coventry: College of Policing, 2014) https://www.college.police.uk/What-we-do/Ethics/Documents/Code_of_Ethics.pdf
⁴ Decision of the Complaints Committee 00844-17 *Moss v The Sun*, https://www.ipso.co.uk/rulings-and-resolution-statements/ruling/?id=00844-17
⁵ Decision of the Complaints Committee 00844-17 *Moss v The Sun* https://www.ipso.co.uk/rulings-and-resolution-statements/ruling/?id=00844-17
⁶ https://www.bbc.co.uk/news/uk-england-sussex-43705388
⁷ https://www.policeprofessional.com/news/sussex-officer-dismissed-for-advertising-himself-as-a-prostitute-while-on-sick-leave/
⁸ Police Oracle https://www.policeoracle.com/pay_and_conditions/police_pay_scales.html
⁹ Sussex Police Federation, 'Reduction in pay' https://www.polfed.org/sussex/advice/sickness-advice/reduction-in-pay/
¹⁰ Valuation Office Agency, 'Private rental market statistics, monthly rents recorded between 1 October 2015 and 30 September 2016 for the South East' https://assets.publishing.service.gov.uk/government/uploads/system/uploads/attachment_data/file/569613/South_East_Maps_17112016.pdf
¹¹ Florence-nightingale.co.uk, 'Nursing & Midwifery: The Nightingale Pledge, 1893' https://www.florence-nightingale.co.uk/the-nightingale-pledge-1893/

Chapter 7

¹ *Time*, 30 March 2018, 'The real reason why Mary Magdalene is such a controversial figure' https://time.com/5210705/mary-magdalene-controversial/
² https://assets.publishing.service.gov.uk/government/uploads/system/uploads/attachment_data/file/936239/victims-code-2020.pdf
³ Crown Prosecution Service, 'Hate Crime' https://www.cps.gov.uk/hate-crime
⁴ Finextra.com, 'UK cash withdrawals plummet 60% during Covid-19 lockdown' https://www.finextra.com/newsarticle/35728/uk-cash-withdrawals-plummet-60-during-covid-19-lockdown
⁵ https://eachother.org.uk/ridiculous-charges-dropped-against-migrant-sex-workers-who-shared-flat/
⁶ National Ugly Mugs, 2019 Impact Report https://uglymugs.org/um/impact-report-201920/
⁷ Beyond the Gaze https://www.beyond-the-gaze.com/
⁸ NPCC (2019), National Policing Sex Work and Prostitution Guidance http://library.college.police.uk/docs/appref/Sex-Work-and-Prostitution-Guidance-Jan-2019.pdf

Postscript

¹ My Doctorate research was funded through a PhD Studentship awarded by Durham University and later honoured at the University of York when I transferred there in 2016.

References

Abrahams, J. and Ingram, N. (2013) 'The chameleon habitus: Exploring local students' negotiations of multiple fields', *Sociological Research Online*, 18(4): 213–26.

Adams, O. (2019) 'Flaws and critics of the nightingale pledge'. Available at: https://www.researchgate.net/publication/331453727_FLAWS_AND_CRITICS_OF_NIGHTINGALE_PLEDGE

Addams, J. (1895) 'The settlement as a factor in the labor movement', in C. Lemert (ed) *Social Theory: The Multicultural and Classic Readings*, Colorado: Wesleyan University, pp 68–70.

Afifi, W. and Caughlin, J. (2006) 'A close look at revealing secrets and some consequences that follow', *Communications Research*, 33(6): 467–88.

Alberti, G., Bessa, I., Hardy, K., Trappmann, V. and Umney, C. (2018) 'In, against and beyond precarity: Work in insecure times', *Work, Employment and Society*, 32(3): 447–57.

Allaboutlaw.co.uk (2020) *Sex Work: The Proposed Legal Models*. Available at: https://www.allaboutlaw.co.uk/commercial-awareness/legal-spotlight/prostitution-the-proposed-legal-models

Anzaldúa, G. (1987) 'To live in the borderlands', PoetryPower.org from *Borderlands-La Frontera. The New Mestiza*. San Francisco, CA: Aunt Lute Books, pp 194–5. Available at: https://powerpoetry.org/content/live-borderlands

Aral, S., Lawrence, J., Tikhonova, L., Safarova, E., Parker, K., Shakarishvili, A. and Ryan, C. (2003) 'The social organization of commercial sex work in Moscow, Russia', *Sexually Transmitted Diseases*, 30(1): 39–45.

Ashforth, B. and Kreiner, G. (1999) '"How can you do it?": Dirty work and the challenge of constructing a positive identity', *Academy of Management Review*, 24(3): 413–34.

Ashforth, B., Kreiner, G. and Fugate, M. (2000) 'All in a day's work: Boundaries and micro role transitions', *Academy of Management Review*, 25(3): 472–91.

Atchison, C. (2010) 'Report on the preliminary findings for Johns' voice: A study of adult Canadian sex buyers', *Canadian Institute for Health Research and the British Columbia Medical Services Foundation*: 1–37.

Baker, L.M., Dalla, R.L. and Williamson, C. (2010) 'Exiting prostitution: An integrated model', *Violence Against Women*, 16(5): 579–600.

Banks, T.L. (2000) 'Colorism: A darker shade of pale', *UCLA Law Review*, 47(6): 1705–46.

Barreto, M. and Ellemers, N. (2003) 'The effects of being categorised: The interplay between internal and external social identities', *European Review of Social Psychology*, 14(1): 139–70.

Barreto, M., Ellemers, N. and Banal, S. (2006) 'Working under cover: Performance-related self-confidence among members of contextually devalued groups who try to pass', *European Journal of Social Psychology*, 36(3): 337–52.

Bartos, J. and Wehr, P. (2002) *Understanding Conflict*, Cambridge: Cambridge University Press.

Beer, D. (2017) 'Envisioning the power of data analytics', *Information, Communication & Society*, 21(3): 465–79.

Beer, D. (2018) 'Zuckerberg told Congress that the solution to the Cambridge Analytica crisis is giving Facebook more power', *Independent* [Blog post]. Available at: https://www.independent.co.uk/voices/mark-zuckerberg-facebook-congress-cambridge-analytica-more-power-a8299156.html

Bentolila, S., Dolado, J.J. and Jimeno, J.F. (2019) 'Dual labour markets revisited', *CESifo Working Papers*, Munich: Munich Society for the Promotion of Economic Research. Available at: https://www.ifo.de/DocDL/cesifo1_wp7479.pdf

Berg, B. van den and Leenes, R. (2010) 'Audience segregation in social network sites', *2010 IEEE Second International Conference on Social Computing*: 1111–16.

Bernstein, E. (2007) 'Sex work for the middle classes', *Sexualities*, 10(4): 473–88.

Bernstein, E. (2010) 'Militarized humanitarianism meets carceral feminism: The politics of sex, rights, and freedom in contemporary antitrafficking campaigns', *Signs*, 36(1): 45–72.

Bernstein, E. (2019) *Brokered Subjects: Sex, Trafficking and the Politics of Freedom*, Chicago, IL: University of Chicago Press.

Bevan, M. (2014) 'A method of phenomenological interviewing', *Qualitative Health Research*, 24(1): 136–44.

Bindel, J. (2018) 'Prostitution is not a job: The insight of a women's body is not a workplace', *The Guardian*. Available at: https://www.theguardian.com/commentisfree/2018/apr/30/new-zealand-sex-work-prostitution-migrants-julie-bindel

Bosanquet, N. and Doeringer, P.B. (1973) 'Is there a dual labour market in Great Britain?', *The Economic Journal*, 83(330): 421–35.

Bourdieu, P. (1986) 'Forms of capital', in J. Richardson (ed) *Handbook of Theory and Research for the Sociology of Education*, New York, NY: Greenwood, pp 241–58.

Bourdieu, P. and Wacquant, L. (1992) *An Invitation to Reflexive Sociology*, Chicago, IL: University of Chicago Press.

Bowen, R. (2013) *They Walk among Us: Sex Work Exiting, Re-entry and Duality*, MA Thesis, Simon Fraser University. Available at: http://summit.sfu.ca/item/12899

Bowen, R. (2015) 'Squaring up: Experiences of transition from off street sex work to square work and duality – concurrent involvement in both – in Vancouver, BC', *Canadian Review of Sociology/Revue canadienne de sociologie*, 52(4): 429–49.

Bowen, R. and O'Doherty, T. (2014) 'Participant-driven action research (PDAR) with sex workers in Vancouver', in C. Snowden and S. Majic (eds), *Negotiating Sex Work*, Minneapolis, MN: University of Minnesota Press, pp 53–74.

Brents, B., Jackson, C. and Hausbeck, K. (2010) *The State of Sex: Tourism, Sex and Sin in the New American Heartland*, London: Taylor & Francis.

Brooks-Gordon, B., Mai, N., Perry, G. and Sanders, T. (2015) *Production, Income, and Expenditure from Commercial Sexual Activity as a Measure of GDP in the UK National Accounts*, Report for the Office for National Statistics (ONS). Available at: https://eprints.bbk.ac.uk/id/eprint/17962/1/17962.pdf

Brouwers, L. and Herrmann, T. (2020) ' "We have advised sex workers to simply choose other options": The response of Adult Service Websites to COVID-19', *Social Sciences*, 9(10): 181.

Bruckert, C. (2012) 'The mark of "disreputable" labour workin' it: Sex workers negotiate stigma', in S. Hannem and C. Bruckert (eds) *Stigma Revisited: Implications of the Mark*, Ottawa: University of Ottawa Press, pp 66–89.

Bruckert, C. and Hannem, S. (2013) 'Rethinking the prostitution debates: Transcending structural stigma in systemic responses to sex work', *Canadian Journal of Law and Society*, 28(1): 43–63.

Bryan, J. (1965) 'Apprenticeships in prostitution', *Social Problems*, 12(3): 287–97.

Bungay, V., Halpin, M., Atchison, C. and Johnston, C. (2011) 'Structure and agency: Reflections from an exploratory study of Vancouver indoor sex workers', *Culture, Health and Sexuality*, 13(1): 15–29.

Campbell, R., Sanders, T., Scoular, J., Pitcher, J. and Cunningham, S. (2018) 'Risking safety and rights: Online sex work, crimes and "blended safety repertoires"', *The British Journal of Sociology*, 70(4): 1539–60.

Carmichael, H. (2020) 'Matt Hancock tells Question Time he couldn't live on sick pay', *The National*, 19 March. Available at: https://www.thenational.scot/news/18319823.matt-hancock-tells-question-time-couldnt-live-sick-pay/

Chaudoir, S. and Quinn, D. (2010) 'Revealing concealable stigmatized identities: The impact of disclosure motivations and positive first-disclosure experiences on fear of disclosure and well-being', *Journal of Social Issues*, 66(3): 570–84.

Chaykowski, R. (2005) 'Non-standard work and economic vulnerability', Canadian Policy Research Network Inc. No. 3. Available at: https://www.researchgate.net/publication/246963600_Non-Standard_Work_and_Economic_Vulnerability

Crenshaw, K. (1991) 'Mapping the margins: Intersectionality, identity politics, and violence against women of color', *Stanford Law Review*, 43(6): 1241–99.

Cruz, K., Hardy, K. and Sanders, T. (2016) 'False self-employment, autonomy and regulating for decent work: Improving working conditions in the UK stripping industry', *British Journal of Industrial Relations*, 55(2): 274–94.

Cunningham, S., Sanders, T., Scoular, J., Campbell, R., Pitcher, J., Hill, K., Valentine-Chase, M., Melissa, C., Aydin, Y. and Hamer, R. (2018) 'Behind the screen: Commercial sex, digital spaces and working online', *Technology in Society*, 55: 47–54.

Cusick, L., Kinnell, H., Brooks-Gordon, B. and Campbell, R. (2009) 'Wild guesses and conflated meanings? Estimating the size of the sex worker population in Britain', *Critical Social Policy*, 29(4): 703–19.

Dalla, R. (2006) ' "You can't hustle all your life": An exploratory investigation of the exit process among street-level prostituted women', *Psychology of Women Quarterly*, 30(3): 276–90.

Day, S. and Ward, H. (2014) 'Approaching health through the prism of stigma: A longer term perspective', in S. Day and H. Ward (eds) *Sex Work, Mobility and Health in Europe*, London: Routledge, pp 161–77.

Dépelteau, F. (2008) 'Relational thinking: A critique of co-deterministic theories of structure and agency', *Sociological Theory*, 26(1): 51–73.

Diduck, A. and Wilson, W. (2003) 'Prostitutes and persons', *Journal of Law and Society*, 24(4): 504–25.

Dodsworth, J. (2014) 'Sex worker and mother: Managing dual and threatened identities', *Child and Family Social Work*, 19(1): 99–108.

Du Bois, W.E.B. (1903) [29 January 2008 ebook #408] *The Souls of Black Folk*, The Project Gutenberg Ebook. Available at: https://www.gutenberg.org/files/408/408-h/408-h.htm

Duggan, M. (2016) 'The "whorearchy"', *Monique Duggan* [blog post]. Available at: https://moniqueduggan.wordpress.com/2016/08/24/the-whorearchy/

Ebaugh, H. (1988) *Becoming an Ex: The Process of Role Exit*, Chicago, IL: University of Chicago Press.

Emirbayer, M. (1997) 'Manifesto for a relational sociology', *The American Journal of Sociology*, 103(2): 281–317.

Englander, M. (2012) 'The interview: Data collection in descriptive phenomenological human scientific research', *Journal of Phenomenological Psychology*, 43(1): 13–35.

English Collective of Prostitutes (ECP) (2019) *What's a Nice Girl Like You Doing in a Job Like This?* Available at: https://www.redpepper.org.uk/whats-a-nice-girl-like-you-doing-in-a-job-like-this/

Fanon, F. (1967) *Black Skin, White Masks*, Finland: Grove Press.

Foucault, M. (1995) *Discipline and Punish: The Birth of the Prison*, New York, NY: Vintage Books.

Freud, S. (2001) 'A special type of choice of object made by men (1910)', in *The Standard Edition of the Complete Psychological Works of Sigmund Freud: Volume 11 (1910): Five Lectures on Psycho-Analysis, Leonardo da Vinci and Other Work*. Available at: https://icpla.edu/wp-content/uploads/2012/10/Freud-S.-1910.-A-Special-Type-of-Choice-of-Object-made-by-Men-Contributions-to-the-Psychology-of-Love-I-Volume-XI-1910-163-176..pdf

Friedman, S. (2016) 'Habitus clivé and the emotional imprint of social mobility', *The Sociological Review*, 64(1): 129–47.

Geertz, C. (1973) *Thick Description: Toward an Interpretive Theory of Culture*, New York, NY: Basic Books.

Ghilarducci, T. and Lee, M. (2005) 'Female dual labour markets and employee benefits', *Scottish Journal of Political Economy*, 52(1): 18–37.

Giddens, A. (1991) *Modernity and Self-identity: Self and Society in the Late Modern Age*, Cambridge: Polity Press.

Gilfoyle, T. (1987) 'The urban geography of commercial sex: Prostitution in New York City, 1790–1860', *Journal of Urban History*, 13(3): 371–93.

Gilfoyle, T. (1992) *City of Eros: New York City, Prostitution, and the Commercialization of Sex, 1790–1920*, New York, NY: W.W. Norton & Co.

Goffman, E. (1959) *The Presentation of Self in Everyday Life*, Garden City: Doubleday.

Goffman, E. (1961) *Encounters: Two Studies in the Sociology of Interaction*, Ann Arbor, MI: Bobbs-Merrill Company.

Goffman, E. (1963) *Stigma: Notes on the Management of Spoiled Identity*, Englewood Cliffs, NJ: Prentice-Hall.

Goffman, E. (1967) *Interaction Ritual: Essay on Face-to-face Behavior*, London: Routledge.

Gould, S. (1978) 'Morton's ranking of races by cranial capacity: Unconscious manipulation of data may be a scientific norm', *Science*, 200(4341): 503–9.

GOV.UK (2018) *Affordable Home Ownership Schemes*. Available at: https://www.gov.uk/affordable-home-ownership-schemes/help-to-buy-isa

Green, J. (2020) *Green's Dictionary of Slang*. Available at: https://greensdictofslang.com/entry/wqjejvy

Gysels, M., Pool, R. and Nnalusiba, B. (2002) 'Women who sell sex in a Ugandan trading town: Life histories, survival strategies and risk', *Social Science & Medicine*, 54(2): 179–92.

Hall, S. (1994) 'Reflections on the encoding/decoding model: An interview with Stuart Hall', in J. Cruz and J. Lewis (eds) *Viewing, Reading, Listening*, Boulder, CO: Westview Press, pp 253–74.

Hall, S. (2011) 'Introduction: Who needs "identity"?', *Semantic Scholar Questions of Cultural Identity*. Available at: https://pdfs.semanticscholar.org/041f/b0a3cf5b18e0ef7d4a549914d8540451d4d0.pdf

Hall, S. and Du Gay, P. (eds) (1996) *Questions of Cultural Identity*, London: Sage.

Ham, J. and Gilmour, F. (2017) '"We all have one": Exit plans as a professional strategy in sex work', *Work, Employment & Society*, 31(5): 748–63.

Harcourt, C. and Donovan, B. (2005) 'The many faces of sex work', *Sexually Transmitted Infections*, 81(3): 201–6.

Hedin, U. and Månsson, S. (2004) 'The importance of supportive relationships among women leaving prostitution', *Journal of Trauma Practice*, 2(3–4): 223–37.

Hemynge, B. (2003) 'Prostitution in London', in R. Matthews and M. O'Neill (eds) *Prostitution: A Reader*, Farnham: Ashgate, pp 213–14.

Herek, G., Widaman, K. and Capitanio, J. (2005) 'When sex equals AIDS: Symbolic stigma and heterosexual adults' inaccurate beliefs about sexual transmission of AIDS', *Social Problems*, 52(1): 15–37.

Hester, M. and Westmarland, N. (2004) 'Tackling street prostitution: Towards a holistic approach', Home Office Research, Development and Statistics Directorate. Available at: http://dro.dur.ac.uk/2557/1/2557.pdf?DDD34+dss4ae+dss0nw+dul0jk

Hester, M., Mulvihill, N., Matolcsi, A., Sanchez, A.L. and Walker, S.-J. (2019) *The Nature and Prevalence of Prostitution and Sex Work in England and Wales Today*, Home Office and the Office of the South Wales Police and Crime Commissioner. Available at: https://assets. publishing.service.gov.uk/government/uploads/system/uploads/ attachment_data/file/842920/Prostitution_and_Sex_Work_Report. pdf

Hill, M. (1993) *Their Sisters' Keepers: Prostitution in New York City, 1830–1870*, Berkeley: University of California Press.

Hill-Collins, P. (1990) 'Black feminist thought in the matrix of domination', in C. Lemert (ed) *Social Theory: The Multicultural and Classical Readings* (3rd ed.), Colorado: Westview Press, pp 535–46.

Hochschild, A. (1979) 'Emotion work, feeling rules, and social structure', *American Journal of Sociology*, 85(3): 551–75.

Hodges, G. (1997) 'Flaneurs, prostitutes, and historians: Sexual commerce and representation in the nineteenth-century metropolis', *Journal of Urban History*, 23(4): 488–97.

Hoigard, C. and Finstad, L. (1992) *Backstreets: Prostitution, Money and Love*, Cambridge: Polity.

Hughes, E.C. (1945) 'Dilemmas and contradictions of status', *American Journal of Sociology*, 50(5): 353–59.

Hughes, E.C. (1958) *Men and Their Work*, Glencoe, IL: Free Press.

Hughes, L. (2001) *The Collected Works of Langston Hughes: The Poems, 1941–1950*, Columbia, MI: University of Missouri Press.

Hunter, M. (2002) ' "If you're light you're alright": Light skin color as social capital for women of color', *Gender and Society*, 16(2): 175–93.

Kaushik, T. (2019) 'For sex workers, mobile phone becomes a double-edged sword', *The Economic Times: Politics*, 23 July. Available at: https://economictimes.indiatimes.com/news/politics-and-nation/for-sex-workers-mobile-phone-becomes-a-double-edged-sword/articleshow/70340750.cms

Kelleher, P. (2020) 'Sex workers' rights group cruelly denied government funding unless it admits sex work "is inherently exploitative"', *Pink News*, 7 August. Available at: https://www.pinknews.co.uk/2020/08/07/ireland-sex-work-alliance-deparment-of-justice-coronavirus-covid-19/

Kempadoo, K. (ed) (1999) *Sun, Sex, and Gold: Tourism and Sex Work in the Caribbean*, Lanham, MD: Rowman & Littlefield.

King, A. (1999) 'Against structure: A critique of morphogenetic social theory', *Sociological Review*, 42(7): 199–227.

Klair, A. (2019) *Zero-hours contracts are still rife – it's time to give all workers the rights they deserve*, Trade Union Congress Blog. Available at: https://www.tuc.org.uk/blogs/zero-hours-contracts-are-still-rife-its-time-give-all-workers-rights-they-deserve

Knox, B. (2014) 'Tearing down the Whorearchy from the inside', *Jezebel: a supposedly feminist website*. Available at: https://jezebel.com/tearing-down-the-whorearchy-from-the-inside-1596459558

Koken, J. (2012) 'Independent female escort's strategies for coping with sex work related stigma', *Sexuality and Culture*, 16(3): 209–29.

Koken, J., Bimbi, D., Parsons, J. and Halkitis, P. (2004) 'The experience of stigma in the lives of male internet escorts', *Journal of Psychology & Human Sexuality*, 16(1): 13–32.

Law, T. (2013) 'Transitioning out of sex work: Exploring sex workers' experiences', in E. van der Meulen, E. Durisin and V. Love (eds) *Selling Sex: Experience, Advocacy, and Research on Sex Work in Canada*, Vancouver: UBC Press, pp 101–10.

Lemert, C. (ed) (2004) *Social Theory: The Multicultural and Classical Readings* (3rd ed.), Colorado: Westview Press.

Levin, S. (2018) 'Sex workers fear violence as US cracks down on online ads: "Girls will die"', *The Guardian* [online] 10 April. Available at: https://amp.theguardian.com/us-news/2018/apr/10/sex-workers-fear-violence-as-us-cracks-down-on-online-ads-girls-will-die

Lowman, J. (2000) 'Violence and the outlaw status of (street) prostitution in Canada', *Violence Against Women*, 6(9): 987–1011.

Lowman, J. and Atchison, C. (2006) 'Men who buy sex: A survey in the greater Vancouver regional district', *Canadian Review of Sociology and Anthropology*, 43(3): 281–96.

Lowman, J. and Fraser, L. (1995) *Violence against Persons Who Prostitute: The Experience in British Columbia*, Technical Report (Canada Department of Justice, Research, Statistics and Evaluation Directorate).

Lucas, A.M. (2005) 'The work of sex work: Elite prostitutes' vocational orientations and experiences', *Deviant Behavior*, 26(6): 513–46.

Mac, J. and Smith, M. (2018) *Revolting Prostitutes: The Fight for Sex Workers' Rights*, London: Verso.

Mai, N. (2009) *Migrants in the UK Sex Industry: First Finding*, July 2009, ISET, London Metropolitan University.

Mai, N. (2013) 'Embodied cosmopolitanisms: The subjective mobility of migrants working in the global sex industry', *Gender, Place and Culture*, 20(1): 107–24.

Månsson, S. and Hedin, U. (1999) 'Breaking the Matthew effect – on women leaving prostitution', *International Journal of Social Welfare*, 8(1): 67–77.

Martin, J. (2003) 'What is field theory?', *American Journal of Sociology*, 109(7): 1–49.

Marx, K. (1844) *Estranged Labour*. Available at: https://www.marxists.org/archive/marx/works/1844/manuscripts/labour.htm

Matthews, R., Easton, H., Reynolds, L., Bindel, J. and Young, L. (2014) *Exiting Prostitution: A Study in Female Desistance*, New York, NY: Palgrave Macmillan.

Mavin, S. and Grandy, G. (2013) 'Doing gender well and differently in dirty work: The case of exotic dancing', *Gender, Work and Organisation*, 20(3): 232–51.

Mayhew, H. (1861) *London Labour and the London Poor: The London Street-folk. Volume II*. London: Griffin, Bohn and Company [Online, digitised by Microsoft Corporation in cooperation with Cornell University Libraries, 2007]. Available at: https://archive.org/details/londonlabourand01mayhgoog

McKay, S., Jefferys, S., Paraskevopoulou, A. and Keles, J. (2012) *Study on Precarious Work and Social Rights*, London: Working Lives Research Institute, London Metropolitan University.

Mcnaughton, C.C. and Sanders, T. (2007) 'Housing and transitional phases out of "disordered" lives: The case of leaving homelessness and street sex work', *Housing Studies*, 22(6): 885–900.

McNeill, M. (2012) 'Whorearchy', *The Honest Courtesan* [blog post] 10 May. Available at: https://maggiemcneill.wordpress.com/2012/05/10/whorearchy/

Mead, G. (1929) 'The self, the I, and the me', in C. Lemert (ed) *Social Theory: The Multicultural and Classical Readings* (3rd ed.), Boulder, CO: Westview Press, pp 224–9.

Mead, G. (1930) 'Cooley's contribution to American social thought', *American Journal of Sociology*, 35(5): 693–706.

Mead, G. H. (1932) *The Philosophy of the Present*, LaSalle: Open Court.

Meltzer, B.M. (2003) 'Lying: Deception in human affairs', *International Journal of Sociology and Social Policy*, 23(6/7): 61–79.

Miano, A. (2017) 'Feminism 101: What is a SWERF?' Available at: https://femmagazine.com/feminism-101-what-is-a-swerf/

Mishra, S. and Neupane, S. (2015) 'Differentiated typology of sex work and implication for HIV prevention programs among female sex workers in Nepal', *Frontiers in Public Health*, 3(36).

Moore, T. (2005) 'A Fanonian perspective on double consciousness', *Journal of Black Studies*, 35(6): 751–62.

Morris, M. (2018) *Incidental Sex Work: Casual and Commercial Encounters in Queer Digital Spaces*. PhD Thesis, University of Durham. Available at: http://etheses.dur.ac.uk/13098/

Musto, J. (2010) 'Carceral protectionism and multi-professional anti-trafficking human rights work in the Netherlands', *International Feminist Journal of Politics*, 12(3–4): 381–400.

Nagesh, A. (2016) 'Police officer sacked for working as a prostitute while on sick leave', *Metro: News*, 23 December. Available at: https://metro.co.uk/2016/12/23/police-officer-sacked-for-working-as-prostitute-while-on-sick-leave-6342397/

Nagle, J. (1997) *Whores and other Feminists*, New York, NY: Routledge.

Nayar, K. (2016) 'Sweetening the deal: Dating for compensation in the digital age', *Journal of Gender Studies*, 26(3): 1–12.

Newton, F. (2020) 'Why sex workers need two phones', *Vice World News*, 7 October. Available at: https://www.vice.com/en/article/889zy3/why-do-sex-workers-need-two-phones

Nursing & Midwifery Council (NMC) (2015) *The Code Professional Standards of Practice and Behaviour for Nurses, Midwives and Nursing Associates*. Available at: https://www.nmc.org.uk/globalassets/sitedocuments/nmc-publications/nmc-code.pdf

NUM (2019) *NUM Response to the Department of Work and Pensions' Inquiry Report into Universal Credit and Survival Sex*. Available at: https://uglymugs.org/um/press-room/num-response-to-the-department-of-work-and-pensions-inquiry-report-into-universal-credit-and-survival-sex/

Ocha, W. and Earth, B. (2013) 'Identity diversification among transgender sex workers in Thailand's sex tourism industry', *Sexualities*, 16(1–2): 195–216.

O'Connell-Davidson, J. (1998) *Prostitution, Power and Freedom*, Ann Arbor, MI: University of Michigan Press.

O'Doherty, T. (2011) 'Criminalization and off-street sex work in Canada', *Canadian Journal of Criminology and Criminal Justice*, 53(2): 217–45.

O'Doherty, T. (2015) *Victimization in the Canadian Off-Street Sex Industry*. PhD Dissertation, Simon Fraser University. Available at: http://summit.sfu.ca/item/16216

Office for National Statistics (2018) 'Statistical bulletin: Wealth in Great Britain Wave 5: 2014 to 2016', *Office for National Statistics: Statistical Bulletin Wealth in Great Britain Wave 5: 2014 to 2016*. Available at: https://www.ons.gov.uk/peoplepopulationandcommunity/personalandhouseholdfinances/incomeandwealth/bulletins/wealthingreatbritainwave5/2014to2016

O'Neill, M. (2007) 'Community safety, rights and recognition: Towards a co-ordinated prostitution strategy?' *Safer Communities*, 6(1): 45–52.

O'Neill, M. (2010) 'Cultural criminology and sex work: Resisting regulation through radical democracy and participatory action research (PAR)', *Journal of Law and Society*, 37(1): 210–32.

O'Neill, M. and Campbell, R. (2010) 'Desistence from sex work: Feminist cultural criminology and intersectionality – the complexities of moving in and out of sex work', in Y. Taylor, S. Hines and M.E. Casey (eds) *Theorizing Intersectionality and Sexuality: Genders and Sexualities in the Social Sciences*, London: Palgrave Macmillan, pp 163–89.

O'Neill, M., Jobe, A., Bilton, C. and Stockdale, K. (2017) 'Peer talk: Hidden stories, a participatory research project with women who sell or swap sex in Teesside'. A way out. Available at: https://www.awayout.co.uk/wp-content/uploads/2017/10/Hidden-Stories.pdf

Orchard, T., Farr, S., Macphail, S., Wender, C. and Young, D. (2012) 'Sex work in the forest city: Experiences of sex work beginnings, types and clientele among women in London, Ontario', *Sexuality Research and Social Policy*, 9: 350–62.

Penney, T.L. (2013) *The Encyclopedia of Criminology and Criminal Justice*. doi:10.1002/9781118517383.wbeccj248.

Pheterson, G. (1993) 'The whore stigma: Female dishonor and male unworthiness', *Social Text*, 37: 39–64.

Phoenix, A. (2014) 'Colourism and the politics of beauty', *Feminist Review*, 108(1): 97–105.

Piscitelli, A. (2007) 'Shifting boundaries: Sex and money in the north-east of Brazil' *Sexualities*, 10(4): 489–500.

Pitcher, J. (2015) 'Sex work and modes of self-employment in the informal economy: Diverse business practices and constraints to effective working', *Social Policy and Society*, 14(1): 113–23.

Pitcher, J. (2018) 'Intimate labour and the state: Contrasting policy discourses with the working experiences of indoor sex workers', *Sexuality Research and Social Policy*, 16: 138–50.

Potterat, J., Rothenberg, R., Muth, S., Darrow, W. and Phillips-Plummer, L. (1998) 'Pathways to prostitution: The chronology of sexual and drug abuse milestones', *Journal of Sex Research*, 35(4): 333–40.

Raguparan, M. (2017) ' "If I'm gonna hack capitalism": Racialized and indigenous Canadian sex workers' experiences within the neo-liberal market economy', *Women's Studies International Forum*, 60: 69–76.

Razack, S.H. (2000) 'Gendered racial violence and spatialized justice: The murder of Pamela George', *Canadian Journal of Law and Society*, 15(2): 91–130.

Reece, R. (2015) 'The plight of the black Belle Knox: Race and webcam modelling', *Porn Studies*, 2(2–3): 269–71.

Roach, J., Wood, K., Cartwright, A., Percy-Smith, B., Rogerson, M. and Armitage, R. (2020) *An Independent Review of the Managed Approach to On-street Sex Working in Leeds 2014–2020*, Safer Leeds and University of Huddersfield. Available at: https://democracy. leeds.gov.uk/documents/s208220/Managed%20Approach%20 Independent%20Review%20Report%20Appendix%20080720.pdf

Rober, P., Walravens, G. and Versteynen, L. (2012) 'In search of a tale they can live with: About loss, family secrets, and selective disclosure', *Journal of Marital and Family Therapy*, 38(3): 529–41.

Rubenhold, H. (2019) *The Five: The Untold Lives of the Women Killed by Jack the Ripper*, Boston, MA: Houghton Mifflin Harcourt.

Rubin, G. (1992) 'Thinking sex: Notes for a radical theory of the politics of sexuality', in C.S. Vance (ed) *Pleasure and Danger: Exploring Female Sexuality*, London: Pandora.

Sanders, T. (2007) 'Becoming an ex-sex worker', *Feminist Criminology*, 2(1): 74–95.

Sanders, T. (2012) 'Policing commercial "sex work" in England and Wales', in P. Johnson and D. Dalton (eds) *Policing Sex*, London: Routledge, pp 135–49.

Sanders, T. and Hardy, K. (2013) 'Sex work: The ultimate precarious labour?', *Criminal Justice Matters*, 93(1): 16–17.

Sanders, T., Connelly, L. and King, L. (2016) 'On our own terms: The working conditions of internet-based sex workers in the UK', *Sociological Research Online:* 21(4): 15.

Sanders, T., O'Neill, M. and Pitcher, J. (2018) *Prostitution: Sex Work, Policy & Politics*, London: Sage.

Scambler, G. (2007) 'Sex work stigma: Opportunist migrants in London', *Sociology*, 41(6): 1079–96.

Scambler, G. and Scambler, A. (1997) 'Conspicuous and inconspicuous sex work: The neglect of the ordinary and mundane', in G. Scambler and A. Scambler (eds) *Rethinking Prostitution: Purchasing Sex in the 1990s*, London; Routledge, pp 105–20.

Schütz, A. (1967) *The Phenomenology of the Social World* (F. Lehnert and G. Walsh, trans.), Chicago, IL: Northwestern University Press (original work published 1932).

Sciortino, K. (2016) 'Sex worker and activist Tilly Lawless, explains the whorearchy', *Slutever.com: Interviews* [blog post] 23 May. Available at: https://slutever.com/sex-worker-tilly-lawless-interview/

Scottish Government (2018) 'Equally Safe: Scotland's strategy to eradicate violence against women'. Available at: https://www.gov.scot/publications/equally-safe-scotlands-strategy-prevent-eradicate-violence-against-women-girls/

Scoular, J. and O'Neill, M. (2007) 'Regulating prostitution: Social inclusion, responsibilization and the politics of prostitution reform', *British Journal of Criminology*, 47(5): 764–78.

Seidler, V. (2018) *Making Sense of Brexit: Democracy, Europe and Uncertain Futures*, Bristol: Bristol University Press.

Shah, S. (2009) 'Sexuality and "the left": Thoughts on intersections and visceral others', *Feminist Scholar Online*, 7(3): 1–11.

Sky News (2018) *I was trained to get Universal Credit Claimants off the phone*. Sky News Online. Available at: https://news.sky.com/story/i-was-trained-to-get-universal-credit-claimants-off-the-phone-11535770

Smart, L. and Wegner, D.M. (1999) 'Covering up what can't be seen: Concealable stigma and mental control', *Journal of Personality and Social Psychology*, 77(3): 474–86.

Snow, D. and Machalek, R. (1983) 'The convert as a social type', *Sociological Theory*, 1: 259–89.

Standing, G. (2016) *The Precariat: The New Dangerous Class*, London: Bloomsbury Academic.

Sterling, A. and Van der Meulen, E. (2018) ' "We are not criminals": Sex work clients in Canada and the constitution of risk knowledge', *Canadian Journal of Law and Society/Revue Canadienne Droit Et Société*, 33(3): 291–308.

Tait, W. (1840) *Magdalenism: An Inquiry into the Extent, Causes, and Consequences, of Prostitution in Edinburgh*, Edinburgh: Leopold Classic Library.

Taylor, S. and Tyler, M. (2000) 'Emotional labour and sexual difference in the airline industry', *Work, Employment and Society*, 14(1): 77–95.

Todorova, M. (1997) *Imagining the Balkins*, Oxford: Oxford University Press.

Trottier, D. (2012) *Social Media as Surveillance: Rethinking Visibility in a Converging World*, Farnham: Ashgate.

TUC (2015) *The Decent Jobs Deficit: The Human Cost of Zero-hours Working in the UK*, Trade Union Congress. Available at: https://www.tuc.org.uk/sites/default/files/DecentJobsDeficitReport_0.pdf

TUC (2020) 'Insecure work: Why decent work needs to be at the heart of the UK's recovery from coronavirus', [online] Trade Union Congress. Available at: https://www.tuc.org.uk/research-analysis/reports/insecure-work-0

UNAIDS (2020) 'Sex workers must not be left behind in the response to Covid-19', April. Available at: https://www.unaids.org/en/resources/presscentre/pressreleaseandstatementarchive/2020/april/20200408_sex-workers-covid-19

Van der Meulen, E., Durisin, E. and Love, V. (2013) *Selling Sex: Experience, Advocacy, and Research on Sex Work in Canada*, Vancouver: UBC Press.

Van Gennep, A. (1960) *The Rites of Passage*, Chicago: University of Chicago Press.

Veenstra, G. and Burnett, P. (2014) 'A relational approach to health practices: Towards transcending the agency-structure divide', *Sociology of Health & Illness*, 36(2): 187–98.

Wacquant, L. (1990) 'Exiting roles or exiting role theory? Critical notes on Ebaugh's "Becoming an Ex"', *Acta Sociologica*, 33(4): 397–404.

Walkowitz, J. (1980) *Prostitution and Victorian Society: Women, Class and the State*, Cambridge: Cambridge University Press.

Walkowitz, J. (1992) *City of Dreadful Delight: Narratives of Sexual Danger in Late-Victorian London*, London: Virago Press.

Walkowitz, J. and Vicinus, M. (1977) *The Making of an Outcast Group Prostitutes and Working Women in Nineteenth-Century Plymouth and Southampton*, [Online June 2011] Cambridge University Press, pp 192–213. Available at: https://www.cambridge.org/core/books/prostitution-and-victorian-society/making-of-an-outcast-group-prostitutes-and-working-women-in-plymouth-and-southampton/B279EAC6AE4ED7C3AC58918864558C49

Wedderburn, M., Bourne, D., Samuels-Dixon, V. and Robinson, N. (2011) 'Study of female sex workers, client types and risk behavior in the sex work industry in Jamaica', PSI. Available at https://www.psi.org/publication/jamaica-2011-study-of-female-sex-workers-client-types-and-risk-behavior-in-the-sex-work-industry-in-jamaica/

White, L. (1990) *The Comforts of Home: Prostitution in Colonial Nairobi*, Chicago, IL: University of Chicago Press.

Zatz, N. (1997) 'Sex work/sex act: Law, labor and desire in constructions of prostitution', *Signs*, 22: 277–308.

Zimmerman, A. (2018) 'Sex workers fear for their future: How SESTA is putting many prostitutes in peril', *Daily Beast*, 4 April. Available at: https://www.thedailybeast.com/sex-workers-fear-for-their-future-how-sesta-is-putting-many-prostitutes-in-peril

Index

effect of Brexit on sex
workers 96–100
European identity, importance of 100
exclusion, violence of 137–43
exiting sex work ('sexiting') 44–5
bidirectionality of 46
and financial hardship 139–40
literature on 35–8, 53
'Managed Area' in Leeds, evaluation
of 149–50
exploitation
in academic environments 28
historical 20, 21
of migrant workers 109
by work/in work 138, 145
zero-hours contract work 40, 133–4

F

Facebook 83, 84, 87–8, 91
Fanon, Franz, 'twoness concept' 59
fear 57, 96, 136–7
feminisation of poverty 20, 134
resistance to 40–1
feminism/feminists 16, 18–19, 20–1,
38–9, 138, 146
financial exclusion 151–2
Finstad, L., off-street sex work 11
*Five, The: The Untold Lives of the
Women Killed by Jack the Ripper*
(Rubenhold) 13
'flexicurity', duality providing 41, 42,
45, 62–3, 131, 134
forced labour in sex industries (survival
sex) 3
FOSTA-SESTA bill (2018), US 85
freedom attained by duality 51–2
freedom of movement and
Brexit 108–10
Freud, Sigmund, Madonna-Whore
dichotomy 101
Friedman, S., *habitus clivé* 65

G

gay male white 23–4
gender pay gap 38, 40
General Data Protection Regulation
(GDPR) 84–5
Gilfoyle, Timothy, 19th-century New
York 13, 102–3
Goffman, E.
actual vs virtual social identity 113
'discrediting' vs 'discreditable'
stigma 113
'double double life' 71–2, 74
dramaturgical model of social life 8,
57, 71, 93
on dualism and concealed stigma 57,
82, 114

'impression management' 28, 72
'matrix of possible events' 8, 46
'selective disclosure' 123–4
government policies 17, 19, 37,
84–5, 148
Graeber, David, 'bullshitization of
academic life' 27–8
'gross misconduct' 140, 141, 142
in-group oppression, sex workers 102
Gysels, M., Uganda study 14–15

H

Habitus (Bourdieu and Wacquant) 26
habitus clivé 65, 74
Hall, Stuart, cultural identities 57–8,
62, 71
Hardy, K., survey of sex workers 16, 27
harvesting of information 82, 83
hate
hate crimes 149
online hate 117–18
Hedin, U., sex work exiting 36
Hemynge, B., prostitution in Victorian
London 13
Herrmann, T., response of ASWs to
Covid-19 146
Hester, M.
charities serving sex workers 155–6
'needs and support' model 37
prevalence of sex work in the
UK 9–10
hierarchies 100–1
colourism as hierarchy of
whiteness 104
UK whorearchy 110–12
whorearchies 101–3
Hill, Marilyn, 19th-century New
York 102
historical context 11–16
class conflict 20–1
whorearchies 102–3
HIV/AIDS 14, 118
Hochschild, A., concept of 'emotion
work/labour' 28, 59
Hodges, G., review of 19th-century
historians 102–3
Hoigard, C., off-street sex work 11
household debt 47–8
Hughes, E.C., taints associated with
different types of work 118
hypocrisies about sex work,
ending 158

I

identification with (sex) work 55–7,
115–16
identity
cultural 57–8, 62